Synthetic Drug Addiction

William Dudley

Addictions

ReferencePoint
Press®

San Diego, CA

© 2015 ReferencePoint Press, Inc.
Printed in the United States

For more information, contact:
ReferencePoint Press, Inc.
PO Box 27779
San Diego, CA 92198
www.ReferencePointPress.com

Picture credits:
Cover: Thinkstock Images
Maury Aaseng: 31–34, 46–49, 60–61, 73–75
© Mills, Andy/Star Ledger/Corbis: 15
© Boris Roessler/epa/Corbis: 11

LIBRARY OF CONGRESS CATALOGING-IN-PUBLICATION DATA

Dudley, William, 1964–
   Synthetic drug addiction / by William Dudley.
     pages cm. -- (Compact research series)
   Audience: Grade 9 to 12
   Includes bibliographical references and index.
   ISBN 978-1-60152-764-6 (hardback) -- ISBN 1-60152-764-0 (hardback) 1. Designer drugs--Juvenile literature. 2. Drug addiction--Juvenile literature. 3. Drugs of abuse--Juvenile literature. 4. Synthetic drugs--Juvenile literature. I. Title.
   RM316.D84   2015
   615.7'8--dc23
                                 2014031739

Contents

Foreword

As modern civilization continues to evolve, its ability to create, store, distribute, and access information expands exponentially. The explosion of information from all media continues to increase at a phenomenal rate. By 2020 some experts predict the worldwide information base will double every seventy-three days. While access to diverse sources of information and perspectives is paramount to any democratic society, information alone cannot help people gain knowledge and understanding. Information must be organized and presented clearly and succinctly in order to be understood. The challenge in the digital age becomes not the creation of information, but how best to sort, organize, enhance, and present information.

ReferencePoint Press developed the *Compact Research* series with this challenge of the information age in mind. More than any other subject area today, researching current issues can yield vast, diverse, and unqualified information that can be intimidating and overwhelming for even the most advanced and motivated researcher. The *Compact Research* series offers a compact, relevant, intelligent, and conveniently organized collection of information covering a variety of current topics ranging from illegal immigration and deforestation to diseases such as anorexia and meningitis.

The series focuses on three types of information: objective single-author narratives, opinion-based primary source quotations, and facts and statistics. The clearly written objective narratives provide context and reliable background information. Primary source quotes are carefully selected and cited, exposing the reader to differing points of view, and facts and statistics sections aid the reader in evaluating perspectives. Presenting these key types of information creates a richer, more balanced learning experience.

For better understanding and convenience, the series enhances information by organizing it into narrower topics and adding design features that make it easy for a reader to identify desired content. For example, in *Compact Research: Illegal Immigration*, a chapter covering the economic impact of illegal immigration has an objective narrative explaining the various ways the economy is impacted, a balanced section of numerous primary source quotes on the topic, followed by facts and full-color illustrations to encourage evaluation of contrasting perspectives.

The ancient Roman philosopher Lucius Annaeus Seneca wrote, "It is quality rather than quantity that matters." More than just a collection of content, the *Compact Research* series is simply committed to creating, finding, organizing, and presenting the most relevant and appropriate amount of information on a current topic in a user-friendly style that invites, intrigues, and fosters understanding.

Synthetic Drugs at a Glance

Synthetic Versus Natural Drugs
Unlike drugs that are extracted or derived from plants or fungi, such as marijuana and cocaine, synthetic drugs are created in chemical laboratories.

Sales of Synthetic Drugs
In recent years synthetic drugs have been created for sale and use as legal substitutes for illicit recreational drugs such as marijuana and MDMA (ecstasy).

Proliferation
As many as three hundred varieties of synthetic drugs are on the market, with more being developed all the time.

Most Common Types
The two types of synthetic drugs that have drawn the most attention are synthetic marijuana (spice) and synthetic stimulants (bath salts).

Health Dangers
Users of synthetic drugs have been hospitalized with various symptoms, including tremors, psychotic breaks, and heart and kidney failure.

Availability
Synthetic drugs are known for being available on the Internet or from convenience stores, tobacco shops, gas stations, and other retail outlets.

Deceptive Labeling

Synthetic drugs are often labeled "not for human consumption" and sold misleadingly as bath salts, potpourri, incense, lens cleaner, or plant food.

Legal Status

Although several dozen of the chemicals used in making synthetic drugs have been banned by federal and state laws, drug makers have been able to continue selling synthetic drugs by slightly altering the chemical formulas they use.

Overview

❝In much of the world, traditional mood-altering substances such as cocaine and heroin are in decline. But a pharmacopoeia of synthetic drugs is rapidly taking their place.❞

—*The Economist*, a British newspaper.

❝Technological advances, market globalization, and the ubiquitous nature of the Internet is likely to generate a continuing flow of cheap psychoactive synthetic drugs for years to come.❞

—Nora D. Volkow, director of the National Institute on Drug Abuse.

In March 2012 Chase Burnett, age sixteen, purchased a packet of Mojo Diamond Extreme Potpourri at a convenience store in Peachtree, Georgia. The athlete and high school honor student took his purchase home, smoked it, and died in his parents' hot tub. Kris Sperry, Georgia's chief medical examiner, later determined that Burnett had no prior health problems and no drugs in his system—except for synthetic marijuana. "He drowned because he was under the influence of one of the synthetic cannabinoids that made him unconscious,"[1] Sperry told the *Atlanta Journal-Constitution*.

Dickie Sanders was a troubled twenty-one-year-old who was trying to get his life back together after problems with marijuana abuse, scrapes with the law, and a stint in drug rehab. At a court-ordered group therapy session, another drug user sold Sanders a packet of "bath salts," telling him it created a high and would not be found in drug tests. Sanders snorted the powdery substance November 10, 2010. Instead of euphoria, he experienced psychotic levels of fear, despondence, and paranoia. A suicide attempt in which he slashed his own throat with a knife left him hospitalized; a later suicide attempt with a gun left him dead.

An Emerging Global Threat

Burnett and Sanders were both victims of what have come to be called synthetic drugs—a term that loosely refers to an emerging class of artificial drugs that mimic some of the properties of more familiar illicit drugs such as marijuana and cocaine. The drug types involved in the deaths of Burnett and Sanders (synthetic marijuana and bath salts) were first detected by the Drug Enforcement Administration (DEA) in 2008. They had been found as early as 2004 in Great Britain and Europe and have also been found in Canada, Australia, and other countries— making them a truly global public health threat. Synthetic drug use has increased greatly in a short time. Synthetic marijuana

> " **Synthetic marijuana was unknown in the United States prior to 2008. By 2011 one in nine high school seniors had reported using it at least once during the previous year.** "

was unknown in the United States prior to 2008. By 2011 one in nine high school seniors had reported using it at least once during the previous year, according to the Monitoring the Future survey of youth drug use. This made it second only to marijuana in popularity among the drugs asked about by the survey—well ahead of cocaine, hallucinogens, and MDMA (ecstasy). Synthetic stimulants have not attained similar popularity, but thousands of people have tried them.

What Are Synthetic Drugs?

Broadly defined, synthetic drugs are drugs that have been artificially created in a laboratory rather than derived from plants. However, in recent years the term has acquired a narrower definition, referring to drugs that became available in the United States after 2008 and share the following characteristics:

- They mimic the effects of well-known psychoactive drugs such as marijuana, LSD, and cocaine.
- They are (or were, when first introduced) legal to possess and consume.
- Their manufacture and sale are unregulated, meaning that a person has no idea of the dosage or exact chemical contents in a given packet, or whether two identically labeled packets of drugs are in fact the same.
- They can be used without being detected in standard drug tests.
- They have been linked to numerous health problems and behaviors, including mental breakdowns and suicide.

How Synthetic Drugs Are Marketed and Sold

Another thing that distinguishes synthetic drugs from other drugs is how they are marketed and distributed. Rather than being sold on the street by a drug dealer, many synthetic drugs can be openly purchased at convenience stories, gas stations, head shops, and other retail outlets. They can also be purchased over the Internet.

Synthetic drugs are often marketed as something other than drugs. Synthetic marijuana is often sold as herbal incense or potpourri, and synthetic stimulants have been sold as plant food or jewelry cleaner. The term *bath salts* has become so popular as to become a generic term for synthetic stimulants. These drugs are often sold in packets labeled "not meant for human consumption" or something similar. However, those who buy and sell these products share an implicit understanding that the products being sold are, in fact, drugs meant to be snorted or smoked for their psychoactive effects.

> " Synthetic drugs are often marketed as something other than drugs. "

Two Main Types

Chemical analyses of synthetic drugs have found numerous chemical combinations and formulas. However, discussions of synthetic drugs

Synthetic marijuana, often sold under the name "spice," can be up to a hundred times more potent than its natural counterpart. Spice and other synthetic marijuana products may produce extreme anxiety and paranoia and even lead to suicidal behavior.

generally focus on one of two types: synthetic marijuana (spice) and synthetic stimulants (bath salts).

Synthetic marijuana consists of dried leaves or other plant matter that has synthetic cannabinoids sprayed on it. Cannabinoids are a family

> **[Synthetic marijuana] can be up to one hundred times more potent than its natural counterpart.**

of chemicals that affect the same parts of the brain as marijuana. Synthetic marijuana resembles natural marijuana in that it is usually smoked or drunk as tea. However, it can be up to one hundred times more potent than its natural counterpart. Commonly called "spice," other popular street names for synthetic marijuana include K2, Bliss, Bombay Blue, and Black Mamba. Synthetic stimulants are made of synthetic derivatives of cathinones, a central nervous system stimulant. These synthetic cathinones are chemically similar to the active ingredients found in cocaine, methamphetamine, and other stimulants. They are generally sold in powder or crystal form (hence the term *bath salts*); sometimes they are sold or consumed as capsules or tablets. They are usually snorted or ingested orally. Common street names for synthetic cathinones include Ivory Wave, Bloom and White Lightning.

Other Synthetic Drugs

Most discussion of synthetic drugs deals with either synthetic cannabinoids or synthetic cathinones. However, some people include in the synthetic drug category other artificially produced drugs developed (or popularized) in the twenty-first century. Examples include Foxy Methoxy (5-MeO-DIPT), a potent hallucinogen, and a family of hallucinogenic drugs called synthetic phenethylamines that go by the street names Smiles, Bromo-Dragonfly, and N-Bomb. Bromo-Dragonfly and others have been blamed for several cases of fatal overdose. Methoxetamine (called "mexxy") has a similar chemical structure to ketamine and PCP (angel dust). Touted as a safe alternative to those controlled substances, mexxy has been especially popular in Europe despite being linked to several deaths. A class of drugs (6-apb and 5-apb) marketed under the name Benzo Fury has been marketed as a legal stimulant/hallucinogen.

Another drug that is sometimes lumped together with synthetic marijuana and bath salts is MDMA, also called ecstasy. MDMA is a synthetic hallucinogen that became popular in the 1980s and 1990s but was classified as an illicit substance in 1985. In recent years a new drug known as

"Molly" became popular with young people at music festivals. Promoted as an especially pure version of MDMA, investigators found that many samples sold as Molly instead contained the cathinones usually sold under different names as bath salts.

How Do Synthetic Drugs Threaten Public Health?

There have been numerous reports of emergency room visits, law enforcement encounters, and injuries and deaths attributed to bath salts and other synthetic drugs. These stories have led health experts to pronounce synthetic drugs as a significant public health challenge.

Part of the public health challenge of synthetic drugs is the fact that relatively little is known about them. Both spice and bath salts have been used as drugs for a relatively short time. There has been little in the way of scientific studies on exactly how they affect the body or on long-term ramifications of chronic use. Most of the available knowledge on synthetic drugs comes from medical and police reports, warnings by public health authorities, and personal observations of drug users and those close to them.

The Effects of Synthetic Marijuana

Synthetic marijuana takes about three to five minutes to take effect, and the duration of its high can be one to eight hours. Various immediate effects on the human body have been reported. These include dilated pupils, sweating, vomiting, tachycardia (fast, racing heartbeat), and elevated blood pressure. An education resource produced by the Partnership at Drugfree.org states that "what may be of the greatest concern is the loss of physical control—a kind of brain-body disconnect."[2] This is manifested in lack of pain response, tremors, and spastic or uncontrolled body movements.

The effects of synthetic marijuana on a person's thoughts and feelings also present possible health dangers. Users may experience dysphoria (a state of feeling unwell or

> **There have been numerous reports of emergency room visitations, law enforcement encounters, and injuries and deaths attributed to bath salts and other synthetic drugs.**

unhappy), which is the opposite of euphoria (feelings of well-being or elation). They may feel extreme emotions of anxiety and paranoia. They may also experience incessant thoughts of suicide or harming others—thoughts that can lead to unfortunate actions.

The Effects of Bath Salts

Bath salts, like other stimulants, primarily affect the central nervous system, which in turn can cause symptoms in other parts of the body. The immediate effects of bath salts on the body include high blood pressure, chest pains, tachycardia, dehydration, and kidney failure. Bath salts are also linked with psychiatric symptoms, including paranoia, hallucinations, and panic attacks. People under the influence of synthetic stimulants often engage in bizarre and violent behavior and are at risk for injuring themselves and others.

> **People under the influence of synthetic stimulants often engage in bizarre and violent behavior and are at risk for injuring themselves and others.**

There have been several cases in which an overdose of synthetic stimulants has proved fatal. In Maine in July 2011, thirty-two-year-old Ralph Willis was arrested and jailed for criminal mischief after running around and yelling at people. He stopped breathing in jail, was transferred to a medical facility, and died. The medical examiner later confirmed that the cause of death was an overdose of MDPV, a common ingredient in bath salts.

There have also been cases in which suicidal thoughts and feelings persist for days, even after other effects of bath salts have subsided. Suicidal thinking and behavior may last "even after the stimulatory effects of the drugs have worn off," says Zane Horowitz, medical director of the Oregon Poison Center. "At least for MDPV there have been a few highly publicized suicides a few days after their use."[3]

The Problem of Drug Addiction

In addition to potential immediate effects that can leave synthetic drug users hospitalized or worse, synthetic drugs may have longer-term im-

Synthetic stimulants, often sold as "bath salts" and labeled "not for human consumption," contain substances that are chemically similar to those found in cocaine and methamphetamine. Bath salts have been linked to paranoia, hallucinations, and violent behavior.

pacts on a person's health. One major concern is their potential to lead to addiction.

Drug addiction occurs when a user reaches a state where the body craves the drug and/or a person feels psychologically compelled to keep using it despite intentions to quit. Cocaine and methamphetamine are two well-known examples of highly addictive drugs. Research has suggested that cocaine and methamphetamine's addictiveness stems from the drugs' effects on neurotransmitters (the chemicals that carry messages in the brain). Both cocaine and methamphetamine (through different mechanisms) raise the levels of the neurotransmitter dopamine in the brain, which in turn stimulates neurons and creates feelings of pleasure. Both drugs interfere with the body's natural production and regulation of dopamine, leading to drug dependence and addiction.

How Addictive Are Synthetic Drugs?

Synthetic drugs have some of the same properties as other addictive drugs. Synthetic stimulants, for instance, affect neurotransmitters in the brain in much the same way as a combination of cocaine and methamphetamine. Studies have shown that bath salts increase the brain's levels of dopamine much like cocaine, but can be up to ten times more potent.

Whether synthetic cathinones are just as addictive as cocaine and methamphetamine—or possibly even more addictive—is unclear. In the absence of scientific studies on their long-term effects, it is impossible at this point to make that determination, but there are strong clues. Some studies in which mice were able to self-administer synthetic stimulants found them acting in ways that strongly suggested addiction. Dirk Hanson, who writes about drug addiction, concludes that "there no longer seems to be much doubt about the stimulant drugs known collectively as bath salts. To a greater or lesser degree, these off-the-shelf synthetic stimulants appear to be potentially addictive. And that's not good news for anyone."[4]

Less is known about the addictive potential of synthetic marijuana. Like with its natural counterpart, some people seem to be able to try spice without becoming addicted, whereas others succumb to chemical dependency. Hanson asserts that "the matter of the addictiveness of spice and other synthetic cannabis products remains open to question."[5] But drug treatment specialist Dr. Howard Samuelson argues that many spice users in his care display classic addiction symptoms. "Spice abusers report cravings of the drug that are extremely compelling and defy the logical portion of their brains, which tells them to abstain," he writes. "Stopping the intake of spice after a period of consistent spice usage invokes unpleasant side effects."[6] These withdrawal symptoms include agitation, tremors, panic attacks, headaches, nausea, and feelings of depression.

Treatment of Synthetic Drug Abuse

Treatment of synthetic drug addiction can vary depending on the specific drug but generally follows the same methods used to treat addiction to other drugs. Treatment often takes place in residential treatment centers staffed with trained medical personnel and counselors. The first step is a detoxification phase. During this step, which can last hours or days, addicts often experience withdrawal symptoms that include tremors, strong cravings for the drug, and physical discomfort. Once withdrawal is completed and these symptoms subside, patients undergo various types of therapy, including individual, group, and family counseling. Sometimes the therapy deals with underlying mental and emotional health problems that predate the patient's addiction. Other therapies focus on teaching basic life and coping skills. These include recognizing situations that trigger drug use, developing relationships with nonusing peers, and learning activities and behaviors to cope with stress other than using drugs.

> " In the United States both the federal government and state governments have passed laws and enacted policies to combat the problem of synthetic drug abuse. "

In dealing with synthetic drug addiction, drug treatment professionals often stress the importance of aftercare and the dangers of relapse. This is especially true for teens, who often face significant pressure from friends to try new kinds of synthetic drugs. David Carlyle, a clinical therapist, says that patients who complete treatment at residential treatment centers should attend daily support group meetings for at least three months and participate in aftercare programs beyond that period. Addicts who "make it," he argues, are those who slowly transition "from inpatient to intensive outpatient-to-outpatient and then at home."[7]

What Government Policies Can Best Combat Abuse of Synthetic Drugs?

Prior to 2010 the chemicals used to make synthetic marijuana and bath salts were legal to possess in the United States. Not only could people sell or purchase synthetic drugs without fear of criminal prosecution, but their manufacture was not regulated or monitored. This is no longer the case. Governments around the world have taken several steps to stop the manufacture, distribution, and consumption of synthetic drugs. Countries in Europe began to outlaw synthetic marijuana in 2009 and synthetic cathinones in 2010. In the United States both the federal government and state governments have passed laws and enacted policies to combat the problem of synthetic drug abuse. In 2010 Kansas became the first state to outlaw the sale and use of certain synthetic cannabinoids used to make synthetic marijuana. That same year Louisiana became the first state to criminalize synthetic cathinones—the chemicals used to make bath salts. Since then the federal government and most other state governments have classified various chemicals that make up synthetic drugs as illegal substances. Similar policies have been enacted in Canada, Great Britain, Australia, and other countries.

A Moving Target

The effort to place synthetic drugs within America's ongoing War on Drugs campaign has been mixed, but there have been some encouraging signs. The growth of synthetic drug use, after exploding from 2009 to 2011, has since leveled off. The number of calls to poison control centers about synthetic marijuana fell from around fifty-two hundred in 2012 to half that number (twenty-six hundred) in 2013. That decline coincided with federal legislation in 2012 that banned many chemicals used to make synthetic drugs.

However, many makers and sellers of synthetic drugs have responded to synthetic drug prohibition by creating new chemicals that are not specifically banned but have similar pharmacological effects. They thus create a moving target that evades legal restrictions. In 2013, one year after President Barack Obama signed the federal law banning twenty-six chemical precursors to synthetic drugs, reporter Emily Ethridge wrote, "There are more than 250 types of synthetic drugs still sold in the United States, according to the Drug Enforcement Agency, and law enforcement can't keep up. The problem is that once a certain substance is banned or restricted, manufacturers can slightly alter the chemical structure of the illicit substance to make a new version that skirts the law."[8] Or, as Senator Charles Grassley noted at a September 2013 Senate hearing, "A change of a molecule or two to a banned drug is sometimes enough to make a new and legal alternative."[9]

Could Legalization Prevent Synthetic Drug Abuse?

Instead of constantly adding new chemicals to the lists of banned substances, some people have called for a radically different approach to synthetic drugs. An alternative policy would be to treat synthetic drugs more like nicotine cigarettes—make them legal but require health warning labels, sales restrictions for minors, and other regulations. New Zealand is one country trying what has been called a harms reduction strategy. Instead of banning synthetic drugs entirely, it permits licensed retailers to sell drugs that have been tested and found to be of low risk.

Some people have called for a relaxation of marijuana laws as a way to reduce synthetic drug use. They argue that natural marijuana, which has been around for thousands of years, is far less harmful than its synthetic equivalents. People who turn to synthetic drugs despite its dangers often do so to avoid positive drug test results and legal ramifications. So legalizing marijuana may turn people away from spice and other synthetic drugs.

Calls for relaxation of drug prohibition laws—whether for synthetic drugs or the drugs for which they substitute—remain controversial. As public health authorities and others scramble to confront the new and evolving threat of synthetic drugs, most would agree with Grassley that these drugs pose "a difficult problem without an easy solution."[10]

What Are Synthetic Drugs?

—Maureen Barrett, who became an antidrug activist after her seventeen-year-old son was found dead with synthetic marijuana in his system.

—Tony O'Neill, who writes about drugs and culture in *Salon*.

Drugs are chemical substances that affect a person's brain and body when ingested. Synthetic drugs are artificial—they are created in chemical laboratories rather than derived from nature, such as from plants or mushrooms. Taken at face value, the term *synthetic drug* can refer to any drug created artificially. Many prescription medications are synthetic drugs. However, by the early 2000s the term acquired a narrower and more ominous meaning. It came to refer to a class of manufactured drugs that mimic the effects of illicit recreational drugs such as marijuana and cocaine but are often sold legally in retail outlets and via the Internet. Other phrases used to describe this class of drugs include *new psychoactive substances* and *synthetic legal intoxicating drugs*.

This narrower definition encompasses many different substances. From 2009 to 2014 the DEA identified between two hundred and three hundred chemicals in synthetic drugs, and new chemicals are constantly being created and introduced. However, most discussions of synthetic drugs have focused on two main categories: synthetic marijuana and synthetic stimulants.

Spice Emerges in Europe

Sometime around 2004 a new type of smokeable herbal product emerged in Europe under the brand name of Spice. It consisted of dried and shredded leaves or other plant material and bore a superficial resemblance to marijuana. It could be smoked like marijuana to get high, and users often reported similar psychoactive effects such as elevated mood, relaxation, and mild sensory distortions. Unlike marijuana, it was legal to possess and did not show up on standard drug tests. Distributed via the Internet and in small retail outlets, by 2008 Spice and competing brands had spread from Europe to other countries, including the United States.

> " From 2009 to 2014 the DEA identified between two hundred and three hundred chemicals in synthetic drugs, and new chemicals are constantly being created and introduced. "

This alternative to marijuana was (and still is) touted as a natural herbal high. However, in late 2007 and 2008, European scientists determined that the marijuana-like properties did not come from the plant materials but from synthetic chemicals that were sprayed on them. These chemicals bind (like a lock and key) to the cannabinoid receptors—the same parts of the brain affected by tetrahydrocannabinol (THC), the main active ingredient in natural marijuana. The THC in marijuana is derived from the cannabis plant; the sprayed-on chemicals in spice are called synthetic cannabinoids.

The Inventors of Synthetic Cannabinoids

Synthetic cannabinoids were actually discovered and developed years and decades before they became popular as spice. Many can be traced to the work of one man—a chemistry professor named John W. Huffman. From 1984 to 2010 Huffman and his team at Clemson University synthesized 450 cannabinoid compounds. The purpose of these compounds was to facilitate scientific research on how brain receptors worked to regulate mood and well-being and to see if drugs similar to THC could be developed to help cancer and AIDS patients. These research chemicals were not intended by Huffman to be used recreationally. However, after he published his research, others took that information and used it to make and market synthetic marijuana.

> " There are some important chemical and pharmacological differences between ordinary pot and its synthetic version. "

The family of chemicals developed by Huffman and his associates are labeled using his initials. Thus, common synthetic cannabinoids found in synthetic marijuana in Europe and the United States in the 2000s include JWH-018, JWH-073, and JWH-398. Another group of synthetic cannabinoids often found in synthetic marijuana was developed in the 1970s by the pharmaceutical firm Pfizer and includes CP 59,540 and CP 47,497 (*CP* stands for company founder Charles Pfizer). HU-210, another synthetic cannabinoid, was first developed at Hebrew University of Jerusalem. These cannabinoids, like those of the JWH family, were not intended for recreational human consumption, but that did not stop people from using them to make synthetic marijuana.

Differences Between Synthetic and Natural Marijuana

Both THC and the cannabinoids found in synthetic marijuana bind with and affect certain cannabinoid receptors in the brain. However, there are some important chemical and pharmacological differences between ordinary pot and its synthetic version.

THC is what is called a partial agonist, whereas synthetic cannabinoids are full agonists. "The difference is important," writes psychiatrist Jason Jerry, "because partial agonists bind to receptors but stimulate them only partially." This limits the risk of an overreaction or an overdose. "In contrast," states Jerry, "full agonists have no ceiling on the dose-response relationship and therefore have a greater potential for overdose and severe toxic effects."[11] This difference may help explain why synthetic marijuana can be ten to eight hundred times more potent than natural marijuana in its binding effects on the brain receptors.

Another difference between natural and synthetic marijuana is cannabidiol (CBD), one of numerous compounds present in marijuana but not in its synthetic version. Research has suggested that both THC and synthetic cannabinoids may increase paranoid delusions and other symptoms of psychosis. However, the CBD in marijuana is believed to have an anxiety-reducing effect and has been shown by some studies to be an effective antipsychotic medication. Many believe this may explain why spice has developed a greater reputation for creating anxiety or psychotic symptoms and why many marijuana users who have tried spice do not like it. "A good number of Spice and K2 users put the drug down because it is too potent," writes Jeffrey Post, a drug testing company executive. "The relaxing and loquacious effects of marijuana smoking have been replaced by agitation and anxiousness."[12]

Synthetic Stimulants Based on Khat

At roughly the same time spice emerged on the drug scene in Europe and the United States, a class of new synthetic stimulants also gained popularity. They were sold as white or brown powder in small packets labeled "not for human consumption" but with the implicit understanding that the crystals could be snorted or otherwise ingested to get feelings similar to what one gets from taking stimulants such as methamphetamine or cocaine. Bath Salts was the name of a particularly popular brand of these stimulants, and the name eventually became a common shorthand name for this type of synthetic drug (which has nothing to do with Epsom salts or other salts one actually puts in bathtub water).

The actual psychoactive chemicals found in Ivory Wave and other popular bath salt brands are called synthetic cathinones. They are related to cathinone, a chemical found in khat (pronounced "cot"), a shrub found in East Africa and the Middle East. For centuries people in that region have chewed khat leaves to experience a sense of elation and alertness. The cathinone in khat, like marijuana, is classified as a drug of abuse that is illegal in the United States.

Synthetic cathinones were first developed in the 1920s and 1930s by scientists and drug firms seeking new medical treatments. Like synthetic cannabinoids, they reemerged much later as recreational drugs. Three synthetic cathinones commonly found in bath salts are MDPV, mephedrone, and methylone. These three chemicals are just a few of the many synthetic cathinones that have the potential to be used or abused as recreational drugs.

The signs of bath salts intoxication can vary depending on what synthetic cathinone is used. Mephedrone produces effects similar to amphetamine and cocaine, whereas MDPV can have effects closer to the hallucinogen MDMA. In general, symptoms of bath salts intoxication include feelings of euphoria, sexual stimulation, mental focus, and high energy for two to four hours. This can be followed by feelings of depression and discomfort for several hours or even days afterward.

Other Drugs Found in Bath Salts

Many packets of bath salts contain chemicals in addition to synthetic cathinones. Sometimes these chemicals may have unpredictable and dangerous effects, especially when used in combination. For example, some brands of bath salts contain lidocaine. Lidocaine is used by dentists as a local anesthetic, but it is used in some bath salts to intensify the drug's effects. Lidocaine overdose has been blamed for some deaths of people taking bath salts.

Some bath salts may not contain synthetic cathinones at all. Analyses of drugs sold as bath salts and spice have increasingly found other kinds of chemicals. Some of them are drugs already familiar as illicit drugs that have been essentially repackaged as a new type of synthetic drug. These include methamphetamine, an addictive stimulant; MDMA, a drug similar to cathinones that has both stimulant and hallucinogenic properties; and PCP, a powerful drug that was popular in the 1980s that often causes violent behaviors. Other chemicals found in synthetic drug packets are not on any banned list of illegal drugs but have similarities to illicit substances. A class of drugs called piperazines, a central nervous system stimulant with effects similar to amphetamine and MDMA, were initially developed as industrial chemicals, but they have also been sold and used as "legal ecstasy."

> " Synthetic cathinones were first developed in the 1920s and 1930s by scientists and drug firms seeking new medical treatments. "

Synthetic Hallucinogens

One type of synthetic drug that has received urgent recent attention are phenethylamine-class hallucinogens. Hallucinogens, the most familiar of which is LSD, are a class of drug that creates severe and profound distortions of a person's perceptions of reality. Synthetic hallucinogens have gone under the name Smiles or N-Bomb, named after its chemical labels (25I-NBOMe, 25C-NBOMe, and others). They sometimes appear as powder in packets or capsules (similar to bath salts) but are also sometimes sold as a liquid soaked into blotter paper.

The natural precursor of these synthetic drugs is mescaline, which has a long history as a hallucinogen. However, the synthetic versions are much more potent than mescaline or LSD. According to the DEA, the "available data suggests that extremely small amounts of these substances can cause seizures, cardiac and respiratory arrest, and death" and that "reports from medical examiners and toxicology labs link some combination of 25I-NBOMe, 25C-NBOMe, and 258-NBOMe to the death of at least 19 individuals, aged 15 to 29 years, in the U.S. between March 2012 and August 2013."[13]

The Unknown Factors

The questions surrounding the exact chemical composition of bath salts underscores the uncertainties that surround synthetic drugs. Since 2004 in Europe and 2008 in the United States, there has been a proliferation of new synthetic drugs. Due to the efforts of law enforcement, the scientific community, health professionals, and academic drug researchers, much more is now known about these drugs. And yet much remains unknown, including the basic question as to what exactly is in a given bag of spice or packet of bath salts.

There are several reasons why that question is so difficult to answer. The manufacture of synthetic drugs may be inconsistent. Spice packets may use different or varied amounts of synthetic cannabinoids. Most labeling and information provided by sellers of synthetic drugs is incomplete or inaccurate. The testing and regulation required for prescription medications in the United States does not apply to synthetic recreational drugs. The White House Office of National Drug Control Policy (ONDCP) has noted that "the contents and effects of synthetic

> **Two packets of synthetic drugs with identical labeling bought weeks or months apart may consist of entirely different chemical combinations.**

cannabinoids and cathinones are unpredictable due to a constantly changing variety of chemicals used in manufacturing processes devoid of quality controls and government regulatory oversight."[14] Finally, synthetic drugs are constantly being invented and reinvented by those who make and sell them. Slight changes are made to the chemistry of the drugs as a way around efforts to make them illegal.

For all these reasons, two packets of synthetic drugs with identical labeling bought weeks or months apart may consist of entirely different chemical combinations; the drug consumer has no way of knowing what exactly he or she is taking. This element of the unknown, in addition to the accumulated stories of synthetic drug abuse, is a big reason why synthetic drugs are considered such a potentially serious problem for the United States and other nations.

Primary Source Quotes*

What Are Synthetic Drugs?

❝In my view, synthetic drugs are diabolical.❞

—Dianne Feinstein, opening statement for Senate Caucus hearing on "Dangerous Synthetic Drugs," September 25, 2013.
www.drugcaucus.senate.gov.

Feinstein is a US senator from California and chair of the Senate Caucus on International Narcotics Control.

❝There is no question that bath salts and spice are both dangerous and poorly-understood kinds of drugs; but it is *how* and *why* they are so dangerous that needs to be clearly understood.❞

—Alan Stevens, *Understanding Addiction to Bath Salts.* Highland Park, NJ: Pomerantz, 2014, p. 5.

Stevens runs a drug rehabilitation center in Palm Beach, Florida, and has written several books on addictive drugs.

* Editor's Note: While the definition of a primary source can be narrowly or broadly defined, for the purposes of Compact Research, a primary source consists of: 1) results of original research presented by an organization or researcher; 2) eyewitness accounts of events, personal experience, or work experience; 3) first-person editorials offering pundits' opinions; 4) government officials presenting political plans and/or policies; 5) representatives of organizations presenting testimony or policy.

❝There are seven different structural categories of synthetic cannabinoids and many variants within groups.❞

—Bryan Wilson, Hamid Tavakoli, Daniel DeCecchis, and Vimutka Mahadev, "Synthetic Cannabinoids, Synthetic Cathinones, and Other Emerging Drugs of Abuse," *Psychiatric Annals*, December 2013, p. 559.

Tavakoli is a psychiatrist at the Naval Medical Center Portsmouth and a professor at Eastern Virginia Medical School. DeCecchis is a psychiatric resident at Naval Medical Center Portsmouth. Wilson and Mahadev are medical students at Eastern Virginia Medical School.

❝Teens and twenty-somethings already fond of pot turn to Spice because it's easy to get, they perceive it as legal, and because schools and sports teams don't test for it.❞

—Melanie Haiken, "Spice and K2 vs. Bath Salts: The Other Designer Drug Scare," *Forbes*, June 13, 2012. www.forbes.com.

Haiken is a health journalist and senior editor for Caring.com.

❝Synthetic marijuana products can be repackaged and sold under many names.❞

—Dr. Tishta Ghosh, quoted in Colorado Department of Public Health and Environment, "Several Synthetic Marijuana Products Identified as Possible Sources of Disease," news release, September 12, 2013. www.colorado.gov.

Ghosh is a public health official who was named interim chief medical officer for the state of Colorado in 2013.

❝Because they are often legal, synthetic drugs may not be perceived as dangerous.❞

—Jennifer Van Pelt, "Synthetic Drugs—Fake Substances, Real Dangers," *Social Work Today*, July/August 2012.

Van Pelt is a health journalist and fitness instructor.

❝Obviously, manufacturers and retailers of these products . . . do not disclose the synthetic drug contents. And for good reason: neither the products nor their active ingredients have been approved by the Food and Drug Administration for human consumption.❞

—Nora D Volkow, statement before the Caucus on International Narcotics Control, United States Senate, September 25, 2013.

Volkow is director of the National Institute on Drug Abuse.

❝One reason that synthetic drugs are extremely dangerous is that buyers don't know what chemicals they are ingesting. Individual products can contain a vast range of different chemical formulations and potencies.❞

—Allegany County Health Department, "Synthetic Drugs," 2014. www.alleganyhealthdept.com.

The Allegany County Health Department provides community services and information for Allegany County in Maryland.

What Are Synthetic Drugs?

- Synthetic drugs are generally sold under misleading names and labels to avoid regulation.

- Synthetic marijuana is frequently labeled "incense" or "potpourri."

- Besides bath salts, synthetic stimulants have been sold as plant food, plant fertilizer, or research chemicals.

- Bath salts sell in small packages of **200 to 500 milligrams** for around twenty dollars a package.

- Synthetic cannabinoids interact with the CB1 receptors of the brain, the same brain receptors affected by marijuana.

- Bath salts are usually snorted through the nose; they can also be smoked, injected, or ingested orally or rectally.

- Synthetic marijuana is usually smoked; it can also be baked into foods such as brownies or made into tea.

- Synthetic drugs, including spice and bath salts, have not been clinically tested on humans, and their consumption has not been approved by the Food and Drug Administration.

- A typical dose of synthetic marijuana can be less than **1 milligram**.

Synthetic Drugs Found by the European Union Early Warning System

The EU Early Warning System is a multinational Europe-based initiative to monitor the introduction of new psychoactive drugs. Most, if not all, of the drugs that have been identified are synthetic drugs. The first synthetic cathinones and synthetic cannabinoids were identified in 2008; since then numerous varieties have been found. In addition, many different kinds of phenethylamines, tryptamines, piperazines, and other unnamed synthetic drugs have been uncovered. Phenethylamines and tryptamines are hallucinogenic drugs that can occur naturally in plants or animals; most emerging drugs of these types are synthesized. Piperazines are synthetic drugs that can create effects similar to amphetamines and MDMA (ecstasy).

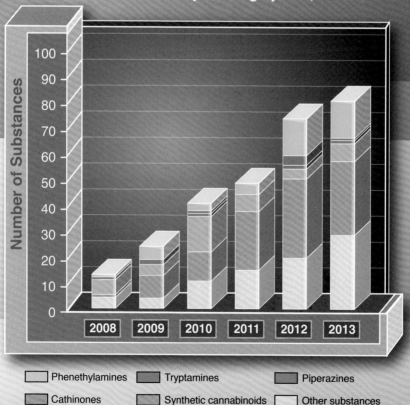

Number and Main Groups of New Psychoactive Substances Notified to the EU Early Warning System, 2008–13

Legend:
- Phenethylamines
- Cathinones
- Tryptamines
- Synthetic cannabinoids
- Piperazines
- Other substances

Source: European Monitoring Centre for Drugs and Drug Addiction, "European Drug Report 2014:Trends and Developments," 2014. www.emcdda.europa.eu.

Two Main Types of Synthetic Drugs

The two main types of synthetic drugs are synthetic cannabinoids and synthetic cathinones. In both categories, a popular brand name (Spice, Bath Salts) evolved into a generic term for the drug.

Type	Example street/brand names	Sometimes sold as	Most common method of ingestion	Speed of onset	Length of high	Reported health effects
Synthetic cannabinoids	K2 Spice Blaze Bliss Black Mamba Bombay Blue Genie Zohai JWH-018	Incense Potpourri	Smoked	3–5 minutes	1–8 hours	Loss of control Lack of pain response Increased agitation Pale skin Seizures Vomiting Profuse sweating Uncontrolled/spastic body movements Elevated blood pressure Heart rate Palpitations Paranoia Delusions
Synthetic cathinones	Bath Salts Cotton Cloud White Lightning White Snow Thunda	Bath salts Insect repellent Plant food Stain remover	Snorted through nose Taken orally	15 minutes	4–6 hours	Suicidal thoughts Agitation Combative/violent behavior Confusion Hallucinations/psychosis Increased heart rate Hypertension Chest Pain Death or serious injury

Source: The Partnership at Drugfree.org, "Synthetic Drugs: Bath Salts, K2/Spice: A Guide for Parents and Other Influencers," February 16, 2012. www.drugfree.org.

Spice and Cannabis: Similarities and Differences

Synthetic marijuana binds to the same parts of the brain as natural marijuana (cannabis), and many of its effects are also commonly observed in cases of natural cannabis intoxication. However, synthetic cannabinoids are also associated with symptoms that are not normally the result of smoking marijuana.

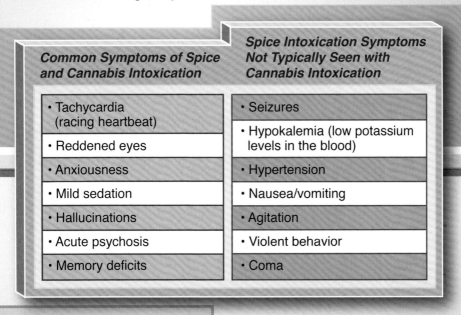

Common Symptoms of Spice and Cannabis Intoxication	Spice Intoxication Symptoms Not Typically Seen with Cannabis Intoxication
• Tachycardia (racing heartbeat)	• Seizures
• Reddened eyes	• Hypokalemia (low potassium levels in the blood)
• Anxiousness	• Hypertension
• Mild sedation	• Nausea/vomiting
• Hallucinations	• Agitation
• Acute psychosis	• Violent behavior
• Memory deficits	• Coma

Source: Beth A. Rutkowski, "Will They Turn You into a Zombie? What Clinicians Need to Know About Synthetic Drugs," 2nd ed., December 3, 2013. www.uclaisp.org.

- Because their ingredients are new and constantly evolving, synthetic drugs generally go undetected in standard urine tests.

- Synthetic marijuana can cost from **$10 to $50** a gram.

- Synthetic marijuana has greater potency (effects on the CB1 receptors) than THC.

- Synthetic cathinones are derived from khat, a naturally occurring substance used for centuries as a psychotropic drug in Africa and the Middle East.

Spread of Synthetic Cannabinoids in the United States

The National Forensic Laboratory Information System (NFLIS) is a program of the Drug Enforcement Administration that collects data from participating state and local forensic labs. The two maps record the number of times the forensic labs detected or identified synthetic cannabinoids. They indicate how synthetic cannabinoids (spice) spread between 2010 and 2012.

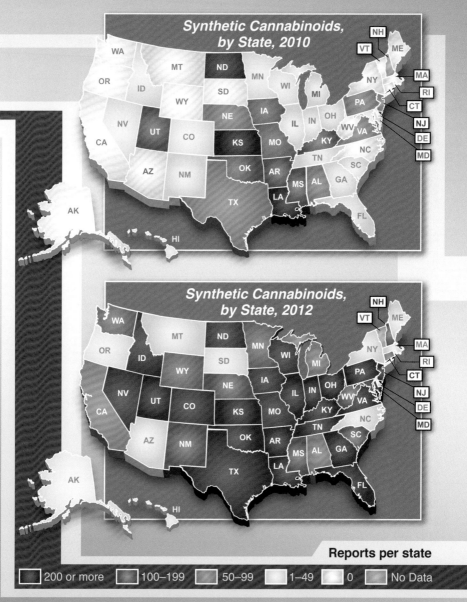

Reports per state

200 or more | 100–199 | 50–99 | 1–49 | 0 | No Data

Source: Substance Abuse Treatment and Mental Health Services Integration Taskforce (SATMHSIT), "Synthetic Drugs: Myths, Facts, and Strategies," February 19, 2013. http://cjcc.dc.gov.

Do Synthetic Drugs Pose a Significant Public Health Threat?

❝I just saw a kid this week . . . who had smoked K2 and was having chest pain, palpitations, headaches and trouble breathing.❞

—Dr. Colin Kane, a pediatric cardiologist at Children's Medical Center in Dallas, Texas.

❝Bath salts can have very harmful effects on its users. Some involve bizarre, violent behavior and tragic outcomes. Users have reported impaired perception, reduced motor control, extreme paranoia and violent episodes.❞

—The American College of Emergency Physicians, a professional organization that represents physicians, residents, and medical students.

In August and September 2013 Colorado experienced a public health outbreak that involved 263 people being rushed to hospitals and treated in emergency rooms (ERs). Many of these patients were highly agitated; some resisted treatment. Fifteen percent of these patients were temporarily placed on ventilators. Most recovered; one person died. The outbreak was serious enough for the Colorado Department of Public Health and Environment to declare an emergency health epidemic, issue a nationwide alert to other doctors, and begin an investigation in cooperation with the national Centers for Disease Control and Prevention.

The cause of this outbreak was not contaminated food or an exotic virus. It was instead a batch of synthetic marijuana. The chemicals had apparently been made in China, imported to Florida where they were sprayed on vegetable matter, then packaged and distributed to stores in Colorado and sold under various names, including Spice, K2, and Black Mamba. It remains unclear why this particular batch of synthetic marijuana proved so dangerous. "Maybe the molecule is a bad one or maybe the concentration was high," notes Dr. Andrew Monte, a researcher at the University of Colorado and Rocky Mountain Poison and Drug Center who investigated the Colorado outbreak. "This is going to continue to be a problem,"[15] he concluded, noting that there was no way to predict when (or where) the next outbreak would strike.

A Public Health Problem

What happened in Colorado was not an isolated incident. Similar spikes in ER admissions due to various synthetic drugs have occurred in Texas, Wyoming, and other states. Nationwide, the number of calls made to poison control centers inquiring about synthetic drugs rose from thirty-two hundred in 2010 to more than thirteen thousand in 2011. The alarming stories and statistics have led most public health officials to conclude that synthetic drugs pose a relatively new public health problem.

Three main factors are behind the worries of health officials. One is that people using synthetic drugs such as spice and bath salts have experienced a variety of serious health effects and even death. Secondly, there have been numerous incidences of drug-induced violent behaviors that endanger both the drug users and the people in proximity to them, including children and first responders. Finally, there is concern that too many people are unaware of or not fully informed about these health risks. Synthetic drugs have an undeserved reputation as being safer than more familiar illicit drugs such as marijuana, cocaine, and heroin.

> "Synthetic drugs have an undeserved reputation as being safer than more familiar illicit drugs such as marijuana, cocaine, and heroin."

Limited Knowledge of Synthetic Drugs

The body of knowledge existing on the health effects of synthetic drugs is somewhat limited. Both spice and bath salts have been used as drugs for a relatively short time. There has been very little in the way of scientific studies of exactly how they affect the body or of their long-term effects. Scientist Jenny Wiley has researched synthetic cannabinoids for years, but admits that "we do not know that much about them, . . . particularly what they do in humans. Many of the compounds that are showing up on the street right now have never been tested on humans."[16]

Until those types of studies can be done, descriptions of the effects of synthetic drugs are most often obtained in the form of anecdotal evidence. These anecdotes come from many sources, including medical case studies, police reports, news stories, and personal observations by drug users and those close to them. Such anecdotal evidence has been deemed reliable enough for public health authorities to issue warnings about synthetic drugs. "Illicit synthetic drugs are dangerous to Florida's children, adults, families and visitors," stated Florida secretary of health John Armstrong in a July 2014 statement. "These drugs destroy lives and threaten public health and safety."[17]

> " There are several health problems associated with synthetic marijuana, especially relating to its effects on the nervous system, lungs, and heart. "

Physiological Effects of Spice

There are several health problems associated with synthetic marijuana, especially relating to its effects on the nervous system, lungs, and heart. Abuse has been linked to several problems with the cardiovascular system. These include rapid heart rate, raised blood pressure, and reduced blood supply to the heart (myocardial ischemia). Spice has also been blamed for heart attacks. In 2010 in Dallas, Texas, three sixteen-year-old boys were hospitalized after suffering what was diagnosed as acute myocardial infarction—a type of heart attack. Dr. Colin Kane, the pediatric cardiologist who treated them, noted that all three of them "were healthy adolescents with no significant past medical history or family history of premature cardiac disease." However, they "gave a history of smoking K2 in the days before the onset of chest pain."[18]

Synthetic marijuana has also been linked to problems with the kidneys, the organs that clean the body's blood. In 2012, for example, clusters of teens in Oregon and Wyoming were hospitalized for kidney failure after smoking spice; at least one teen had to undergo emergency dialysis after his kidneys totally shut down. Synthetic marijuana has also been linked with strokes, seizures, and convulsions. Finally, there may well be harm from smoking the plant material used to make synthetic marijuana, including lung damage.

Physiological Effects of Bath Salts

Bath salts have also led to surges in ER visits and health problems for those who try them. The nervous system stimulation they create can stress and harm the body's cardiac system, leading to symptoms such as chest pain, rapid heartbeat, and elevated blood pressure. Other physiological effects include insomnia, sweating, tinnitus (ringing in the ears), nosebleeds, nausea, and stomach cramps. Science writer David DiSalvo compares taking bath salts to driving one's car at abnormally fast speeds mile after mile "and hoping your engine doesn't explode."[19]

More severe physiological effects are possible in the event of an overdose of bath salts. Bath salts can vary widely in potency, increasing the chances of such an accidental overdose. Overdosing on synthetic stimulants may create rhabdomyolysis (a rapid breakdown of muscle tissue), kidney or liver failure, seizures, and respiratory distress. People who try bath salts often experience a sharp increase in body temperature (up to a life-threatening 108°F, or 42°C). Synthetic stimulants have been listed as a cause of death on multiple occasions. According to the National Institute on Drug Abuse (NIDA), "Intoxication from several synthetic cathinones including MDPV, mephedrone, methedrone, and butylone has proved fatal in several instances."[20]

Effects on Mental Health

In addition to effects on the body, both synthetic marijuana and synthetic stimulants are tied with serious mental health problems and effects. These can range from mild to severe. Mild effects include a drug-induced high, irritability, energy fluctuations, and mood swings. More serious effects include severe panic attacks, agitation, and hallucinations. Both spice and bath salts have been linked with cases of paranoia, delusions, and psychotic breaks that can cause violent behavior against oneself or others. "Users [of bath salts] have reported impaired perception, reduced motor control, extreme paranoia and violent episodes,"[21] according to the American College of Emergency Physicians.

> **Both spice and bath salts have been linked with cases of paranoia, delusions, and psychotic breaks that can cause violent behavior against oneself or others.**

In some instances, the mental illness symptoms reported by synthetic drug users last for weeks or months after the drugs were first taken. In one case study, Vikas Mangewala and three other doctors from a pediatric mental health center in Ohio describe a fifteen-year-old patient who was forcibly taken to the ER by police after barricading himself in his room. He admitted smoking marijuana laced with bath salts. The teen boy was treated for paranoia and released after several days. However, he continued to exhibit signs of paranoia and psychosis; one month later he was referred to Mangewala for inpatient psychiatric care. Mangewala and his colleagues report:

> During initial interview, the patient was noted to have extreme periods of psychomotor retardation [slowdown of physical activity] during which he was nonverbal. At other times, he appeared confused, repeating questions to himself. He would make paranoid statements, such as, "Don't let them take me!" and "How do I get out of this?" . . . He reported that his father was replaced by an imposter and his sister would be harmed by unknown people."[22]

The patient's psychotic symptoms eventually subsided with medication, and he was sent back home. Mangewala and his peers believed that bath salts, rather than marijuana, were to blame for his condition. They state, "Our patient's psychotic symptoms were not present during previous marijuana use and seemed related to acute bath salts use, with full and sustained resolution upon discontinuation. This suggests a primary role for bath salts in producing acute psychosis."[23]

Bizarre Behaviors

The psychosis and other mental health disturbances created by synthetic drugs result in sometimes bizarre acts that not only could harm drug users themselves, but others around them, including family members and law enforcement personnel. For example, in June 2012 a woman in Munnsville, New York, known to be a user of bath salts, had to be subdued by police when she stripped off her clothes, choked her three-year-old child, threatened neighbors, and choked and tried to bite a dog. People on synthetic drugs often turn violently aggressive, increasing risks for first responders, according to Dr. Paul Adams of Jackson Memorial Hospital in Miami, Florida. He explains, "It's dangerous for the police. It's dangerous for the fire fighters. It's dangerous for the hospital workers taking care of them because they [ER patients on synthetic drugs] come in, they have to be restrained both chemically and physically and you're asking for someone to get hurt."[24]

A fact sheet prepared by the American College of Emergency Physicians relates several stories about drug-induced actions that endangered others. One incident involved an Illinois teen who smoked synthetic marijuana and then crashed his car into the bedroom of a two-year-old (the child fortunately was not in the room). Another incident involved an adult male who had taken bath salts and then "attacked his girlfriend's children because he believed they were demons who were attacking him."[25] He had to be subdued by police after trying to attack the children with pepper spray.

Public Health Challenges

Several additional factors make synthetic drugs a major public health challenge. One is the fact that many of these novel drugs are not well known to doctors, making it more difficult for them to accurately diagnose and treat patients. Doctors' response is further hindered by the lack of drug tests such as those that exist for marijuana, cocaine, and other, more familiar drugs of abuse. "Clinically useful diagnostic screens are not available for many of these substances at this time," wrote Teri

Moser Woo and coauthors in a 2013 journal article aimed at pediatricians. Doctors therefore have to develop "a high index of suspicion for use of easily available illicit substances"[26] in order to recognize and treat cases of synthetic drug use.

Another complication is the persistent belief that synthetic drugs (especially those still legal) are somehow safer than marijuana and other illegal drugs. "Every time the public's perception of risk decreases, the use of the drug increases," observes Ruben Baler of the National Institute on Drug Abuse. "It's very important that people understand that these drugs are anything but benign."[27]

> **Synthetic drug packets purchased at stores or online seldom if ever give an accurate listing of their ingredients and concentrations.**

In addition to marketing their wares as safe and natural, makers of synthetic drugs often change or substitute chemicals in an effort to evade drug laws or simply cut costs. These changes are rarely, if ever, noted on packaging. Indeed, synthetic drug packets purchased at stores or online seldom if ever give an accurate listing of their ingredients and concentrations. "At best, users are guessing at dose and have no idea what is actually in the package," says David Ferguson, a professor of medicinal chemistry. "The potential for an overdose is high."[28]

All of these factors contribute to the ongoing public health threat of synthetic drugs—a threat many believe will extend well into the foreseeable future. Andrew Monte, author of a study on the 2013 Colorado outbreak, believes that similar outbreaks "are likely to keep happening. . . . We need better testing to identify these substances, open communication with public health officials when outbreaks occur and we need to make sure physicians ask patients the right questions about their drug use."[29]

Do Synthetic Drugs Pose a Significant Public Health Threat?

Primary Source Quotes

> **❝For both the individuals using them and the general public, so-called designer drugs like 'bath salts,' 'K2' or 'spice' quickly have become a public health crisis.❞**
>
> —Harry Leider, "Seeking Higher Ground: The Dangers of Designer Drugs," *Scientific American*, January 22, 2013.
>
> Leider is a doctor and chief medical officer at Walgreens.

> **❝Is bath salts an epidemic? No, nowhere close. The real drug epidemic is oxycodone, which is now the second highest cause of accidental death in the U.S.❞**
>
> —Melanie Haiken, "'Bath Salts' a Deadly New Drug with a Deceptively Innocent Name," *Forbes*, June 4, 2012. www.forbes.com.
>
> Haiken is a journalist who writes about health and family issues.

Bracketed quotes indicate conflicting positions.

* Editor's Note: While the definition of a primary source can be narrowly or broadly defined, for the purposes of Compact Research, a primary source consists of: 1) results of original research presented by an organization or researcher; 2) eyewitness accounts of events, personal experience, or work experience; 3) first-person editorials offering pundits' opinions; 4) government officials presenting political plans and/or policies; 5) representatives of organizations presenting testimony or policy.

66 **Synthetic drugs like Spice, K2, and 'bath salts' are a serious threat to the health and safety of young people throughout America.** 99

—Gil Kerlikowske, quoted in Office of National Drug Control Policy, "Readout of White House Drug Policy Director Kerlikowske's Meeting with Public Health and Safety Officials on the Emerging Threat of Synthetic Drugs," February 16, 2012. www.whitehouse.gov.

Kerlikowske served as the director of the ONDCP under President Barack Obama from 2009 to 2014.

66 **Emergency physicians treat patients every day who have ingested synthetic drugs. They present with a variety of different symptoms associated with synthetic drug use, including chest pain, elevated blood pressure, nausea, erratic heartbeat, agitation, paranoia, muscle breakdown and/or hypothermia.** 99

—The American College of Emergency Physicians, "Synthetic Drugs Fact Sheet," 2012. http://newsroom.acep.org.

The American College of Emergency Physicians is a professional organization that represents physicians, residents, and medical students.

66 **The majority of [1,898 reviewed] cases [of spice exposures] were in young men intentionally abusing spice. Most exposures resulted in non-life-threatening effects not requiring treatment.** 99

—Christopher O. Hoyte et al., "A Characterization of Synthetic Cannabinoid Exposures Reported to the National Poison Data System in 2010," *Annals of Emergency Medicine*, October 2012. www.sciencedirect.com.

Hoyte is an assistant professor of medicine at the University of Colorado–Denver.

66 **Psychosis is particularly characteristic of spice after prolonged and heavy usage. The incidence of psychosis might be attributable to the absence of cannabidiol in synthetic blends.** 99

—Bryan Wilson, Hamid Tavakoli, Daniel DeCecchis, and Vimutka Mahadev, "Synthetic Cannabinoids, Synthetic Cathinones, and Other Emerging Drugs of Abuse," *Psychiatric Annals*, December 2013, p. 560.

Tavakoli is a psychiatrist at the Naval Medical Center Portsmouth and a professor at Eastern Virginia Medical School. DeCecchis is a psychiatric resident at Naval Medical Center Portsmouth. Wilson and Mahadev are medical students at Eastern Virginia Medical School.

66 Mental/emotional reactions [to bath salts] may include anger, agitation, paranoia, hallucinations, panic attacks, insomnia, and psychotic or combative behavior. Paranoid behaviors and delusions may last for days after the high is over. 99

—Kirsten Anke, "Bath Salts—What's in a Name?," Army Knowledge Online, February 28, 2014. www.army.mil.

Anke is a nurse for the US Army Public Health Command.

66 If marijuana can cause ischemic stroke, and if anything pot can do spice can do better, neurologists will likely encounter increasing numbers of spice-associated strokes in the years ahead. 99

—Dr. John C.M. Brust, quoted in University of South Florida, "New Research Links Smoking Synthetic Marijuana with Stroke in Healthy, Young Adults," ScienceDaily, November 19, 2013. www.sciencedaily.com.

Brust is a professor of clinical neurology at Columbia University College of Physicians and Surgeons.

66 The dangers of bath salts are compounded by the fact that these products may contain other, unknown ingredients that may have their own harmful effects. 99

—NIDA, "Bath Salts," *Drug Facts*, November 2012. www.drugabuse.gov.

NIDA is an agency of the US Department of Health and Human Services.

66 The most dangerous aspect of the synthetic drug [spice] is that it is legal (in some places) and marijuana is not. This is interpreted by some people, including children, to mean that these 'herbal blends' are okay to smoke and that they are a safe alternative to the illegal substance marijuana, when in reality, these chemicals might be much more dangerous. 99

—Meghan Connor, Vanessa Powel, and Chelsea Tennariello, "Students Warned over Synthetic Marijuana Dangers," *Long Island Report*, December 18, 2012. http://longislandreport.org.

Connor, Powel, and Tennariello were students at Hofstra University and reporters/editors for the student-run multimedia *Long Island Report*.

Facts and Illustrations

Do Synthetic Drugs Pose a Significant Public Health Threat?

- According to a report by the Substance Abuse and Mental Health Services Administration (SAMHSA), out of **2.5 million ER visits** that involved drug abuse or misuse in 2011, bath salts were responsible for **23,000** of those visits.

- According to SAMHSA, **67 percent** of the ER visits linked to bath salts also involved patients who used bath salts in combination with other drugs.

- In 2010 synthetic cannabinoids led to more than **11,000 emergency department visits**, with **75 percent** of those visits involving patients aged twelve to twenty-nine.

- Medical examiners in the state of Florida recorded **4,159 deaths** in the first six months of 2013 in which toxicology tests revealed the presence of drugs. Of those cases, **77 deaths** (less than 2 percent) involved synthetic drugs.

- According to the American Association of Poison Control Centers (AAPCC), there have been an average of **245 synthetic marijuana exposures** a month reported to poison centers over the first seven months of 2014.

Emergency Department Visits Involving Synthetic Cannabinoids and Bath Salts

Data on emergency room visits is often used to monitor potential threats to public health. The two graphs break down data on emergency department visits in 2011 compiled by the Drug Abuse Warning Network (DAWN). They show that a majority of the 28,531 visits involving synthetic marijuana consisted of patients with no other drugs in their system. However, many of the 22,904 visits in which bath salts were a factor involved other drugs in combination.

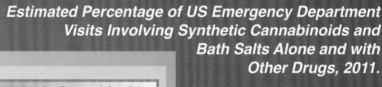

Estimated Percentage of US Emergency Department Visits Involving Synthetic Cannabinoids and Bath Salts Alone and with Other Drugs, 2011.

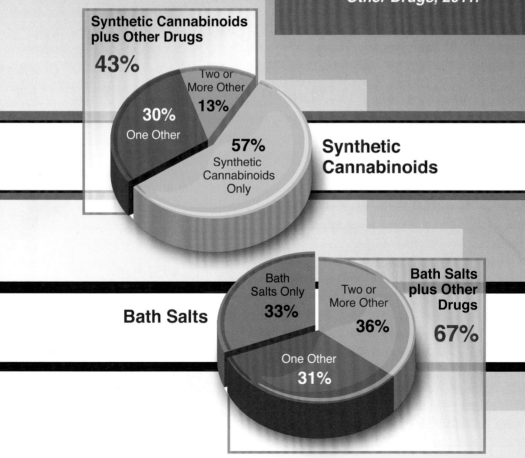

Synthetic Cannabinoids plus Other Drugs
43%

Two or More Other
13%

30%
One Other

57%
Synthetic Cannabinoids Only

Synthetic Cannabinoids

Bath Salts

Bath Salts Only
33%

Two or More Other
36%

Bath Salts plus Other Drugs
67%

One Other
31%

Source: Center for Substance Abuse Research, "More than Half of Synthetic Cannabinoid-Related Emergency Department Visits Involve No Other Drugs; Bath Salt–Related VIsits More Likely to Involve Multiple Substances," October 7, 2010. www.cesar.umd.edu.

Bath Salts–Related Calls to Poison Control Centers Have Fallen

According to data compiled by the American Association of Poison Control Centers, the number of calls placed to poison control centers involving bath salts has declined since peaking in 2011. Possible reasons for the decline include growing public awareness of bath salts and laws making bath salts illegal.

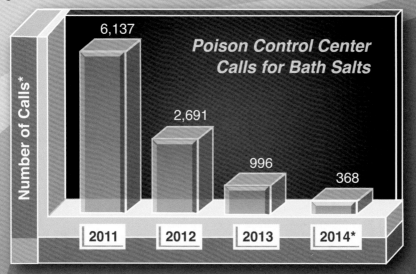

Poison Control Center Calls for Bath Salts

* Numbers through July 31, 2014.

Source: American Association of Poison Control Centers, "Bath Salts Data," July 31, 2014. https://aapcc.s3.amazonws.com.

- According to the AAPCC, there have been an average of **52 bath salts exposures** called in each month to poison control centers over the first seven months of 2014.

- In August 2014 New Hampshire governor Maggie Hassan declared a public health emergency for her state after more than **40 people** were hospitalized after ingesting synthetic marijuana sold under the name "Smacked."

Why Synthetic Drugs Are Dangerous

The chemistry of synthetic drugs varies as do the effects they have on their users. However, all synthetic drugs marketed for recreational use share certain characteristics that make them a potential public health threat.

Problems with All Synthetic Drugs

- Marketed to teens and young adults

- Easily attainable in retail environments and via the Internet

- Unknown ingredient(s)

- No consistency in manufacturing process

- Not tested for human consumption / Unknown short- and long-term effects

- No known dosage—not FDA approved

- Synergistic effects likely when mixed with other drugs or alcohol

Source: Substance Abuse Treatment and Mental Health Services Integration Taskforce (SATMHSIT), "Synthetic Drugs: Myths, Facts, and Strategies," February 19, 2013. http://cjcc.dc.gov.

- In February 2014 North Carolina's public health agency issued an alert warning against acetyl fentanyl ("China White"), a synthetic narcotic linked to three deaths in that state in addition to dozens of deaths in other states.

- In January 2012 motion picture actress Demi Moore was hospitalized for seizures after friends told 911 operators that she had smoked something "similar to incense"; many believe she had been smoking synthetic marijuana, or spice.

Use of Synthetic Marijuana in High School Declines

According to the University of Michigan's Monitoring the Future study, use of synthetic marijuana, or spice, dropped among all surveyed grade levels from 2012 to 2013. The most dramatic drop was among high school seniors.

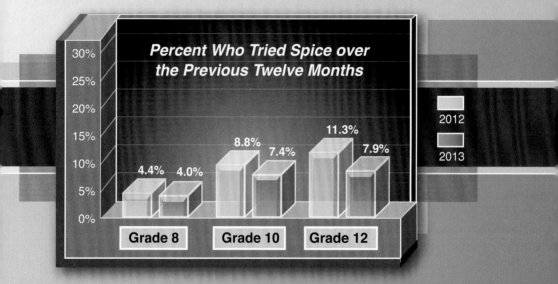

Source: L.D. Johnston, P.M. O'Malley, R.A. Miech, J.G. Bachman, and J.E. Schullenberg. *Monitoring the Future National Results on Drug Use: 1975–2013: 2013 Overview, Key Findings on Adolescent Drug Use.* Ann Arbor: Institute for Social Research, The University of Michigan. www.monitoringthefuture.org.

- Benzodiazepines are the medications commonly used to treat agitation or seizures in patients who have taken either bath salts or spice.

How Addictive Are Synthetic Drugs?

❝Bath salts users have reported that the drugs trigger intense cravings (or a compulsive urge to use the drug again) and that they are highly addictive. Frequent consumption may induce tolerance, dependence, and strong withdrawal symptoms when not taking the drug.❞

—NIDA, an agency of the US Department of Health and Human Services.

❝We haven't seen enough patients yet to ascertain for certain whether tolerance, dependence, or obsessive-compulsive-like use develops with these synthetics.❞

—Jason Jerry, a staff doctor with the Cleveland Clinic.

Kelly (not her real name) first tried synthetic marijuana on her first Halloween after graduating from high school; she says she experienced "an instant and incredible high."[30] She continued to sample it occasionally after that first experience and eventually began taking it on a regular basis—even while studying to be a nurse in college.

> We started smoking and smoking and I kept missing class. My apartment turned into a disgusting mess. I had no desire to clean or do my homework. I would go to work feeling like complete crap. I even would come to work high. . . . I would roll my little spice joints and smoke them like a cigarette waiting for the bus for work. 3 months later I stopped going to college. I dropped out.

. . . My brain was fighting itself for some peace. I couldn't handle myself anymore. I quit. I couldn't sleep at night for at least a week, random sweats, and hot flashes . . . 6 months later I started smoking again.[31]

Most people would classify Kelly's story as a classic case of drug addiction. Although the immediate health effects of synthetic drugs have garnered most of the attention from the media and medical community, there has also been mounting concern over the longer-term problem of addiction.

Differing Opinions

There are some differing views over the addictive potential of synthetic drugs, especially regarding synthetic marijuana. The Drug Policy Alliance, an organization that lobbies for drug policy reforms, including legalization, has claimed that synthetic marijuana is not addictive. "There is no evidence that humans are susceptible to psychological or physiological dependence on or addiction to K2."[32] NIDA, on the other hand, states that "users [of K2] may experience withdrawal and addiction symptoms."[33] Regarding bath salts, Zane Horowitz, medical director of the Oregon Poison Center, concedes, "We don't know if they are addictive. We have not had enough long-term experience with it."[34] However, researchers have found striking chemical and pharmacological similarities between known addictive drugs such as cocaine and the synthetic cathinones found in bath salts. These similarities and numerous anecdotal reports support the idea that bath salts have a high potential for creating addiction.

> " Researchers have found striking chemical and pharmacological similarities between known addictive drugs such as cocaine and the synthetic cathinones found in bath salts. "

Defining Drug Addiction

To understand and evaluate the addictive potential of synthetic drugs, it is important to clarify what people mean by *addiction*. The definition of drug addiction in US society has changed over time. Nora D. Volkow, head of NIDA, writes that in the 1930s, "people addicted to drugs were thought to be morally flawed and lacking in willpower."[35] Viewed in this light, users such as Kelly would be criticized for having poor character and exhibiting poor judgment. In later decades such judgmental attitudes were tempered by the theory that drug addiction was a chemical dependency that created unpleasant physical symptoms after withdrawal (such as Kelly's insomnia and sweating).

More recently, addiction has been defined in terms of persistent and dysfunctional behaviors rather than a moral failing or mere physical ailment. In the context of drug use and abuse, addiction is defined as a brain disorder manifested by involuntary cravings and compulsive behaviors. The American Society of Addiction Medicine defines it as "a primary, chronic disease of brain reward, motivation, memory and related circuitry" that results in individuals "pathologically pursuing reward and/or relief by substance abuse."[36] In this context, a diagnosis of drug addiction for Kelly might note her continuing use of drugs while neglecting cleanliness and schoolwork.

Thus, examining how addictive synthetic drugs are involves several different questions. Do synthetic drugs cause physical dependency? Can they create compulsive and harmful behaviors? How do they affect chemicals in the brain?

Physical Dependency

Many people still equate drug addiction with a physical dependency on drugs, and many cases of drug addiction do feature some form of dependency. This can manifest itself in two ways. A drug user develops a tolerance for a certain drug, meaning that higher doses are required to achieve the same effect. Stopping use of the drug can also create withdrawal symptoms. Both effects are created by the bodily changes resulting from chronic drug use, and both tolerance and withdrawal are signs doctors use to diagnose drug addiction. Noted examples of drugs creating dependency are alcohol and opiates such as heroin.

Do synthetic marijuana or synthetic stimulants create tolerance or withdrawal pains? Answering this question is hampered by the fact that synthetic drugs are a relatively new phenomenon, and very few medical studies have been designed to examine their addictive potential. Jason

Jerry, a staff doctor at the Cleveland Clinic, has spoken and written about the health dangers of synthetic drugs. However, regarding addiction, he acknowledges that "we haven't seen enough patients yet to ascertain for certain whether tolerance, dependence, or obsessive-compulsive-like use develops with these synthetics."[37] However, numerous observations by doctors, treatment counselors, and drug users themselves lend support to the idea that users of synthetic drugs may develop a tolerance for them and may well suffer from withdrawal symptoms—although these symptoms are perhaps not as severe as those for alcohol or opiates.

Withdrawal Pains

A case history involving a patient in Germany who smoked Spice Gold (an early popular brand of synthetic marijuana) every day for eight months suggests that the drugs do cause dependency. According to the patient, growing tolerance of the drug made him triple his daily dosage from 1 to 3 grams to achieve similar results. He was eventually hospitalized, and during his stay doctors observed several symptoms that included anxiety, drug craving, nightmares, sweating, tremors, headaches, and nausea. These symptoms peaked within a week after withdrawal and then subsided. The doctors concluded that physical withdrawal syndrome was their best interpretation of the symptoms, especially since the patient described having similar experiences previously when he went without the drug for a few days and said he only felt better once he had resumed smoking Spice Gold.

> A case history involving a patient in Germany who smoked Spice Gold (an early popular brand of synthetic marijuana) every day for eight months suggests that the drugs do cause dependency.

Withdrawal symptoms have also been observed in people who are trying to stop using bath salts. These symptoms may include depression, anxiety, inability to concentrate or sleep, gastric distress, hallucinations, delirium (sudden and severe onset of confusion), and amnesia.

Addiction and Harmful Behaviors

Not everyone who tries synthetic drugs develops tolerance or a physical dependency on them. However, this does not necessarily mean these individuals avoid the risk of addiction. A person can be diagnosed as being addicted if he or she exhibits certain behaviors. According to the fifth edition of the American Psychiatric Association's *Diagnostic and Statistical Manual of Mental Disorders*, a diagnosis of addictive disorder must meet certain criteria; two to three criteria indicate a mild disorder, four to five criteria indicate a moderate disorder, and six or more indicate a severe disorder. Some of the criteria appear below:

- Tolerance
- Withdrawal symptoms
- Craving or a strong desire to use substance
- Continued use of drug despite knowing it harms one's personal health
- Continued use of drug despite harm to relationships
- Failure to manage work, school, or other responsibilities because of drug use
- Loss of control; taking the drug more or longer than planned
- Unsuccessful attempts or efforts at cutting back or stopping drug use
- Spending significant time obtaining or thinking about the drug
- Reduced involvement in social and occupational activities due to the drug

Thus, a person could still be diagnosed with a drug addiction without exhibiting tolerance or withdrawal symptoms.

Many of these behaviors indicative of addiction have been observed in people who use synthetic drugs. Kelly used synthetic marijuana for months at a time at the cost of her studies and personal cleanliness. Brendan Bickley, executive director of Treatment Solutions Network in California, has treated patients who could not control their drug use. "When I talked to my patients about Spice," he told a journalist, "every one of them would say the effects were extremely unpleasant and they wanted to stop. But then they'd take it again. That was when I realized the addictiveness of the drug."[38]

Similar experiences have been recounted or observed among bath salts users. Hanna, a twenty-one-year old who shared her story with a television news program, told of how she kept using bath salts despite experiencing frightening hallucinations. Her weight dropped to 83 pounds (38 kg), and she left her job and her ballet hobby. "I don't even know why it was so addicting to me, but I just had to keep doing it,"[39] she said. Alan Stevens, CEO of a drug treatment center in Palm Beach, Florida, reports that "bath salt users frequently speak of the compulsive need to continue doing the drug to prolong the experience of the high, resulting in binges that can last for several days."[40]

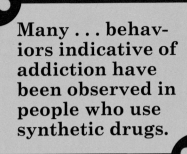

Many . . . behaviors indicative of addiction have been observed in people who use synthetic drugs.

In addition to observations of drug addicts and counselors, evidence for the addictive nature of bath salts and other synthetic drugs has been found in some animal experiments. One noted 2013 study looked at how rats behaved when given doses of methamphetamine as compared to others given the stimulant MDPV, a common ingredient in bath salts. Scientists at the Scripps Research Institute in San Diego set up an apparatus in which rats were able to dose themselves intravenously by pressing a lever a number of times. "Rats are easily 'addictable' as humans are, so they make a good model system to study the behavioral and neurologic effects of these drugs,"[41] writes health writer Alice G. Walton. In this case the scientists increased the number of times rats had to press the lever to get a hit of either MDPV or methamphetamine. They found that rats tended to give up after sixty presses of the lever for methamphetamine, but they averaged six hundred presses to get MDPV. Scientists calculated that rats would work ten times harder to get MDPV, suggesting that its addictive potential is far greater than that of methamphetamine.

Effects on the Brain

In researching drug addiction, some scientists study how drugs (including synthetic drugs) affect the brain. Much of this research focuses on the chemicals used by the brain cells (neurons) to communicate with each other and regulate brain functions. Scientists have identified various neurotransmitters that affect a person's mood. The neurotransmitter dopamine is associated with feelings of pleasure. Noradrenaline affects energy levels, attentiveness, and responsiveness. Serotonin regulates mood, sleep, and memory functions.

Cocaine and methamphetamine are two well-known addictive drugs that work by creating excess levels of dopamine in the brain's synapses (the spaces between neurons). Methamphetamine causes brain cells to release high levels of dopamine into the synapses. Cocaine, on the other hand, inhibits the normal process of reabsorbing the dopamine molecule back into the cells. The net result in both cases is higher levels of dopamine neurotransmitters stimulating brain cell after brain cell, creating an energy rush. When the body's natural production and regulation of dopamine is upset, this can lead to the crash people experience when the drug wears off.

> " Bath salts may combine the effects of methamphetamine and cocaine in a way that may make bath salts even more addictive than those two drugs. "

Scientists researching the synthetic cathinones found in bath salts have found that they also significantly affect neurotransmitter levels. Mephedrone and methylone, two popular synthetic cathinones, have been found to stimulate the brain's release of serotonin and (to a lesser extent), dopamine, in a way similar to amphetamines. MDPV, another cathinone, prevents cells from taking in dopamine. In fact, studies have suggested it is ten times more powerful than cocaine. The net result is that many bath salts may combine the effects of methamphetamine and cocaine in a way that may make bath salts even more addictive than those two drugs.

The Risks of Addiction

Not everyone who tries drugs, including bath salts or spice, becomes addicted to them. Scientists are still trying to figure out what combination of genetics, environment, preexisting mental health issues, and a drug's effects creates addiction. However, the documented experiences of synthetic drug users, the fact that synthetic drugs often produce powerful highs and cravings, and the ongoing research into how synthetic drugs affect brain chemistry all lead to the conclusion that their potential risk for addiction is significant.

How Addictive Are Synthetic Drugs?

66 The combination of strong cravings, insomnia and symptoms like headache or nausea can make synthetic marijuana withdrawal tough to get past. 99

—John Lee, "Synthetic Marijuana Withdrawal: Strategies for Coping with Common Symptoms," www.choosehelp.com, June 23, 2014.

Lee writes about mental health and addiction and is editor of the website Choose help.com.

66 There is no evidence that humans are susceptible to psychological or physiological dependence on or addiction to K2. The potential for harm and abuse is low. 99

—Drug Policy Alliance, "K2/Spice: Establish Regulations But Don't Criminalize It," 2010. www.drugpolicy.org.

The Drug Policy Alliance is an organization that promotes reforms with the goal of reducing what it views as harms caused by drug prohibition.

66 When I started smoking herbal incense, I never thought it was addictive or going to cause me any problems. . . . Two years and over $20,000 later, I couldn't have been more wrong. 99

—JB, "How I Became Addicted and Finally Quit Smoking Herbal Incense," Spice Addiction Support, March 3, 2014. http://spiceaddictionsupport.com.

JB is a husband and father who has struggled with spice addiction.

Bracketed quotes indicate conflicting positions.

* Editor's Note: While the definition of a primary source can be narrowly or broadly defined, for the purposes of Compact Research, a primary source consists of: 1) results of original research presented by an organization or researcher; 2) eyewitness accounts of events, personal experience, or work experience; 3) first-person editorials offering pundits' opinions; 4) government officials presenting political plans and/or policies; 5) representatives of organizations presenting testimony or policy.

66It is not known whether 'bath salts' are addictive. But because they produce many of the same effects as other stimulants such as cocaine and meth, they are likely to be addictive.99

—Government of Canada, "Bath Salts," August 14, 2013. http://healthycanadians.gc.ca.

The official website of the national government of Canada provides health and safety information for Canadian residents and health professionals.

....

66Although the rate of bath salt addiction is reported to be low, several users and former users have admitted to developing a strong, constant urge to use bath salts every day.99

—Mark M. McGraw, "Is Your Patient High on Bath Salts?," *Nursing*, January 2012, p. 29.

McGraw is a critical care staff nurse for the emergency department at the Christiana Care Health System in Newark, Delaware.

....

66We observed that rats will press a lever more often to get a single infusion of MDPV [found in bath salts] than they will for meth, across a fairly wide dosage range.99

—Michael A. Taffe, quoted in Scripps Research Institute, "Scripps Research Institute Team Shows 'Bath Salts' Stimulant Could Be More Addictive than Meth," news release, July 10, 2013. www.scripps.edu.

Taffe is an associate professor at the Scripps Research Institute in San Diego.

....

66I never thought that any kind of substance could control my life the way bath salts ended up controlling it.99

—Hanna, quoted in Sharon Kay, "Woman, 21, Shares Her Struggle to Overcome Addiction to Bath Salts," KCAL9 news, October 26, 2012. http://losangeles.cbslocal.com.

Hanna, a California teenager who was using bath salts up to ten times a day for a fourteen-month period and shared her story of addiction and recovery for a local television news report.

....

Facts and Illustrations

How Addictive Are Synthetic Drugs?

- Drug addiction can involve both physical and psychological symptoms of discomfort when withdrawing from the substance.

- When drugs create artificially high levels of dopamine, the brain adapts by producing less dopamine and reducing its number of dopamine receptors in its reward circuit, reducing a person's ability to feel pleasure in general.

- Withdrawal symptoms from spice (such as internal unrest, cravings, and sweating) generally begin **2 to 3 days** after use is discontinued, peak after **4 to 7 days** of abstinence, and may last up to **3 weeks**.

- Withdrawal symptoms from bath salts can include fatigue, hunger, irritability, and sleeping difficulties.

- Some of the symptoms of synthetic drug toxicity and addiction, such as anxiety and hallucinations, are similar to those of mental disorders such as schizophrenia and bipolar disorder.

- According to NIDA, approximately **9 percent** of people who use marijuana may become dependent. This risk goes up to about **17 percent** of those who start using as adolescents, and **25 to 50 percent** of daily users.

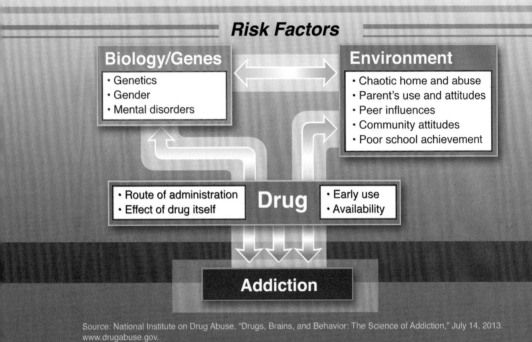

Multiple Risk Factors for Addiction

Not everyone who tries synthetic drugs becomes addicted. There are multiple risk factors that create drug addiction in a person beyond the chemical itself. These include a person's biological characteristics and environmental factors.

Risk Factors

Biology/Genes
- Genetics
- Gender
- Mental disorders

Environment
- Chaotic home and abuse
- Parent's use and attitudes
- Peer influences
- Community attitudes
- Poor school achievement

Drug
- Route of administration
- Effect of drug itself
- Early use
- Availability

Addiction

Source: National Institute on Drug Abuse, "Drugs, Brains, and Behavior: The Science of Addiction," July 14, 2013. www.drugabuse.gov.

- Synthetic marijuana acts on the same brain receptors as natural marijuana; however, there is not enough data yet to ascertain whether synthetic marijuana has similar addiction rates as natural marijuana.

- According to Closing the Addiction Treatment Gap initiative (CATG), about **23 million people** in the United States are addicted to alcohol and/or other drugs.

- According to CATG, **1 in 10 Americans** over the age of 12 (or **23.5 million people**) suffer from some form of addiction. Of these, only about **10 percent** receive addiction treatment.

Parts of the Brain with High Concentrations of Cannabinoid Receptors

The THC in cannabis and the synthetic cannabinoids in spice derive their effects by binding with the brain's cannabinoid receptors. Such receptors are concentrated in various parts of the brain, illustrated here, that regulate different mental, emotional, and bodily functions. Of these structures, the amygdala, hippocampus, and nucleus accumbens are especially linked with drug addiction.

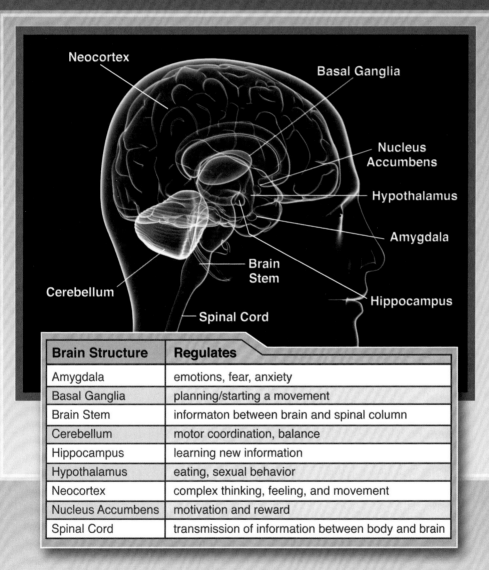

Brain Structure	Regulates
Amygdala	emotions, fear, anxiety
Basal Ganglia	planning/starting a movement
Brain Stem	informaton between brain and spinal column
Cerebellum	motor coordination, balance
Hippocampus	learning new information
Hypothalamus	eating, sexual behavior
Neocortex	complex thinking, feeling, and movement
Nucleus Accumbens	motivation and reward
Spinal Cord	transmission of information between body and brain

Source: Scholastic, Inc., "The Science of the Endocannabinoid System: How THC Affects the Brain and the Body," 2014. www.headsupscholastic.com.

How Should Government Combat Use of Synthetic Drugs?

66The Synthetic Drug Abuse Prevention Act of 2012 . . . placed many of these synthetic drugs on Schedule I, making them illegal. That was an important step to help protect our young people from the effects of these drugs.99

—Charles Grassley, a Republican senator from Iowa.

66Prohibition [of synthetic drugs] is . . . counterproductive in protecting young people as it takes them from buying these products at a corner store or smoke shop and sends them to the cocaine dealer to get them, completely unregulated and unmonitored.99

—Daniel Francis, executive director of the Retail Compliance Association, a lobby for convenience and smoke stores.

The US government's response to the introduction of spice and bath salts as recreational drugs has generally been to place them in the same legal category as the drugs they mimic. The framework of federal drug policy has been the federal Controlled Substances Act (CSA), which Congress passed in 1970 by combining existing federal drug laws into a comprehensive statute. Synthetic drugs such as bath salts and spice were not around in 1970 and thus were not specified in that law, meaning they were not illegal when they were first introduced in America. However, in recent years the US government has used provisions of the CSA to make many popular synthetic drugs illegal—which in turn means it is possible to prosecute both users and sellers. In addition, as of 2014 virtually every state had passed laws outlawing at least some synthetic drugs. Federal agencies, schools, and local police departments have also added spice, bath salts, and other synthetic drugs to their ongoing public education efforts meant to discourage people (especially youth) from trying these drugs.

The Controlled Substances Act

Federal government policy on drugs is governed by a framework established by the CSA. The law established five "schedules" under which drugs are classified; these schedules also determine the level of regulation for each drug. Schedule I drugs are those that present high risk for addiction and serve no recognized medical purpose; sales and possession are banned by law. Schedule II, III, IV, and V drugs are classified on a descending scale of risk for addiction; they also have potential medical use and may be made legal via a doctor's prescription.

The chemicals in spice and bath salts were thus legal because they were not listed in the original CSA classifications. Since then many—but not all—have been placed in Schedule I. Such a designation makes all federal laws against illicit drugs applicable to them.

Placing Synthetic Drugs in Schedule I

The CSA, which has been amended several times since 1970, establishes various procedures for deciding how to classify drugs. The process of determining the appropriate schedule for a given drug includes scientific investigations, done jointly by the DEA and the Food and Drug Administration. Congress can also place drugs in Schedule I directly by legislation. Both of these methods can take a long time; in 1984 Congress gave the US attorney general the power to temporarily place drugs in Schedule I to prevent imminent hazards to public safety.

Both Congress and the attorney general have acted to place synthetic drugs in Schedule I in recent years. In 2011 Attorney General Eric Holder used this authority to temporarily place five synthetic cannabinoids and three synthetic stimulants in Schedule I. In 2013 he acted to place three more synthetic cannabinoids and methylone in Schedule I. By law such placements last a maximum of three years. Congress made most of Holder's designations permanent with the passage of the Synthetic Drug Abuse Prevention Act of 2012, which was signed by Barack Obama in July of that year. The law placed fifteen synthetic cannabinoids, nine synthetic psychedelics, and the synthetic cathinones mephedrone and MDPV in Schedule I.

The Problem of Synthetic Drug Copycats

In all, more than thirty chemicals used for synthetic drugs have been placed on the federal list of banned substances. However, this list is far from complete. A problem noted by many is that illicit drug makers can synthesize chemicals that are chemically similar (but not identical) to prohibited drugs. Thus, they can continue to make and sell drugs that may (or may not) have similar effects, while remaining on the safe side the law. "This is a way for people in the illegal drug market to try and stay one step ahead of the law, by altering the chemical compound of these synthetic drugs to make new drugs that aren't identified yet,"[42] says Bruce Goldberg of the San Francisco office of the DEA.

> A problem noted by many is that illicit drug makers can synthesize chemicals that are chemically similar (but not identical) to prohibited drugs.

The DEA and federal prosecutors have attempted to use 1986 legislation known as the Controlled Substances Analogue Enforcement Act to deal with newly invented synthetic drugs that are not specifically listed in Schedule I. The act states that a "controlled substance analogue shall, to the extent intended for human consumption, be treated, for the purposes of any Federal law as a controlled substance in schedule I."[43] An analogue designation requires proof that the chemical is substantially similar in its molecular structure to a chemical already listed in Schedule I; that it affects the body and brain in ways similar to a Schedule I drug and is represented or intended for use for these similar effects.

The wording of the law has complicated efforts to apply federal criminal laws against synthetic drugs that have been slightly altered by the drug maker. Federal drug cases often turn into battles of expert witnesses as to whether a certain chemical is in fact substantially similar to a banned substance. Synthetic drugs are invariably labeled "not for human consumption," placing the burden on prosecutors to prove otherwise. These hurdles make "investigation and prosecution of analogues . . . far more difficult than that of controlled substances," writes law student Hari Sathappan. "What this means is that prosecution, with its limited resources, may need to let some . . . cases slip through the cracks."[44]

State and Local Approaches

Much of the enforcement of laws against synthetic drugs lies beyond the scope of the federal government. Most states and many municipalities have added synthetic drugs to their own laws against trafficking, selling, and possession of illicit drugs.

State and local governments have tried various legal solutions to combat synthetic drugs. The state of New York added dozens of chemicals to its listing of banned synthetic substances. Kentucky, Rhode Island, and other states have instead banned entire classes of drugs. John Femino, past president of the Rhode Island Society of Addiction Medicine, says that Rhode Island's broad definition approach makes it "much harder for minor re-formulations to continue to be distributed through legal retail channels."[45]

> **Most states and many municipalities have added synthetic drugs to their own laws against trafficking, selling, and possession of illicit drugs.**

In July 2014 Alaska passed a law that banned the sale of drugs based on their packaging rather than their specific chemical formula. It outlawed drugs with "false or misleading" labels that did not specify ingredients. It also banned packaging that suggests that "the user will achieve euphoria, a hallucination, [or] mood enhancement."[46] The state was authorized to cite violators and impose fines (similar to what occurs with traffic tickets) on individuals who sold or possessed the outlawed drugs. The law was inspired by a municipal code in Anchorage that was credited for removing spice and other synthetic drugs from retail outlets.

Questioning the War on Synthetic Drugs

Despite their Schedule I status and federal, state, and local efforts to ban them, synthetic drugs continue to be readily available. Many have wondered whether a different kind of drug policy should be considered. Drug policy analyst Grant Smith argues that simply adding more synthetic drug chemicals to Schedule I "won't impact demand and it certainly won't address the fact that this drug market will remain accessible to anyone who wants in."[47] Criminalization, critics say, drives synthetic drugs to the black market. Smith proposes that a better way of combating synthetic drug abuse would be to treat these drugs like tobacco, which is legal but still subject to regulations. According to Smith, "Product labeling requirements, as well as marketing, branding and retail display restrictions, are proven to reduce youth access to tobacco products and impulse tobacco purchases among adults. This approach is working for tobacco, and could work for synthetic drugs."[48]

> " Criminalization, critics say, drives synthetic drugs to the black market. "

The New Zealand Example

Although many countries in the world have adopted prohibition policies similar to those in the United States, one nation has attracted attention by considering something along the lines of what Smith proposes. In 2013 New Zealand passed a law requiring retailers of drugs meant for nonmedical use to obtain a government license and only sell those drugs that have been tested for safety and found to be of relatively low risk for health problems and addiction. Licensed retailers have limits on advertising, cannot sell to minors, and must clearly and accurately label the chemicals in their products. Writing in 2013, criminal policy expert Eric E. Sterling stated that the goal of this approach was to ensure relative safety for consumers who buy the drugs. "When people choose to consume synthetic drugs non-medically, they will have confidence that there have been studies of the risks and confidence that the purity of manufacture has been confirmed by government inspection."[49]

Under New Zealand's law, forty-one synthetic drugs, including several types of synthetic marijuana, were given probationary legal status. However, early results of the experiment were mixed. The number of outlets selling illicit drugs fell from 4,000 to 110—and all agreed to comply with the new regulations. However, thousands of New Zealanders signed petitions opposing the law, arguing that the legalized drugs were causing addiction and other harms. In May 2014 the government rescinded the legal status of the synthetic drugs it had previously permitted, saying the drugs would have to go through safety testing as provided by the law. The New Zealand law still stands, but over its first year no one has stepped forward to develop clinical testing protocols or perform safety tests on synthetic drugs.

Synthetic Drugs and Marijuana

Marijuana's Schedule I status may also have an impact on synthetic drug use. Synthetic drugs are for the most part undetectable in routine drug screening. This may make them more attractive to people subjected to drug testing, such as drug treatment patients, those on parole or probation, or even teens concerned about drug testing performed by their parents. "The irony is that the only reason that people use synthetic marijuana is because the real thing is illegal,"[50] argues Smith. Removing the illegal status of marijuana, Smith and others believe, may well result in fewer people turning to spice or other synthetic drugs, which they believe are more harmful. "If our government is truly dedicated to protecting public health, it should be making an effort to inform the public about the fact that marijuana is far less harmful than these synthetic products,"[51] argues Mason Tvert, a spokesperson for a Colorado-based group that supports legalized marijuana.

Not everyone agrees that the way to discourage people from using synthetic drugs is to encourage them to use marijuana instead. Many opponents of marijuana legalization argue that both natural and synthetic marijuana are harmful, especially for young people who might infer that legalization signifies safety. Any growing acceptance of marijuana is "a dangerous trend," argues medical writer Elaine Gottlieb, "as new advances in developmental neuroscience show that adolescent brains are differentially vulnerable to the neurotoxic effects of cannabis."[52] Gottlieb and others argue that marijuana use is linked with depression, hallucinations, addiction, and other harms that are also found with synthetic marijuana.

Public Education Efforts

Although a few states have taken steps to legalize marijuana, there is no indication that the United States will follow New Zealand's example and decriminalize synthetic drugs anytime soon. But even those who support synthetic drug prohibition acknowledge that it will not work without public education efforts. "While law enforcement and scheduling legislation play a huge role in addressing this scourge, the complexities of the problem make prevention, education, and treatment invaluable," writes Francesca Liquori, counsel with the National Association of Attorneys General. "Particular care must be taken to educate young adults, parents, first responders, healthcare workers, and retailers."[53]

With the help of funding from the ONDCP, numerous communities have undertaken various initiatives to raise public awareness about the dangers of synthetic drugs. Schools have revised antidrug curriculum materials to include information about spice and bath salts. Community education programs have taught parents how to identify synthetic drugs and their symptoms.

Efforts have also been made to educate retailers. In September 2013 the DEA sent a letter to the top one hundred corporate retail and gas station chains informing them of dangerous synthetic drugs and requesting their cooperation in removing such drugs from their stores. Similar outreach campaigns have been done by states and cities, including programs in Indiana and Illinois that successfully persuaded retailers to stop selling and even turn in their stocks of synthetic drugs.

> **Even those who support synthetic drug prohibition acknowledge that it will not work without public education efforts.**

These education programs in combination with federal and state laws banning synthetic drugs have had some success in combating synthetic drug abuse. After peaking in 2012, use of synthetic drugs among young people continued to decline for the next two years. However, the profitability of the drug trade and the ability of drug criminals to synthesize new chemicals indicates that synthetic drugs will remain a serious problem for the foreseeable future.

How Should Government Combat Use of Synthetic Drugs?

❝We need to…place strong criminal penalties on the sale or possession of 'bath salts' and synthetic marijuana.❞

—John J. Flanagan, "Senators Call on Assembly to Pass Tough Bill on Bath Salts and Synthetic Marijuana," press release, June 14, 2012. www.nysenate.gov.

Flanagan is a New York state senator.

❝As legislators ban more and more harmless chemicals, there will be nothing left but truly dangerous chemicals to ingest. Then kids will be dying. Because kids are going to get high. Always have, always will.❞

—Sally Oh, "Synthetic Marijuana Deaths: Statistically Zero," *Kentucky Free Press*, June 9, 2013. www.kyfreepress.com.

Oh is a Kentucky writer, activist, and founding member of the Lexington Tea Party.

Primary Source Quotes

❝With federal Bureau of Prisons facilities already operating well above capacity, I am concerned that adding new substances to the list of federally banned drugs will further exacerbate overcrowding problems in our federal prisons.❞

—Rand Paul, letter to Senators Charles Grassley and Amy Klobuchar, *Politics* (blog), *Louisville (KY) Courier-Journal*, December 14, 2011. http://blogs.courier-journal.com.

Paul was elected senator from Kentucky in 2010 and opposed the 2012 Synthetic Drug Abuse Prevention Act.

❝In order to meet the emerging threat of synthetic drugs, we must continue to apply a holistic approach to the problem. . . . We must inform sellers and users about the illegality and dangerousness of these substances, and find additional ways to augment our enforcement work with education and prevention.❞

—Timothy J. Heaphy, prepared statement for hearing on "Dangerous Synthetic Drugs," Senate Caucus on International Narcotics Control, September 25, 2013. www.drugcaucus.senate.gov.

Heaphy is US attorney for the western district of Virginia.

❝Synthetic drugs are marketed towards young adults, with brand names like 'Mr. Smiles' and 'Moon Rocks.' While these substances are typically labeled 'not for human consumption,' they are marketed as legal and safe alternatives to controlled substances.❞

—Francesca Liquori, "Designer Drugs Lead to Designer Legislation," *NAAGazette*, February 28, 2014. www.naag.org.

Liquori is counsel for the National Attorneys General Training and Research Institute.

66 Legitimate herbal incense products are clearly labeled 'Not for Human Consumption.' However, if American citizens voluntarily choose to buy and consume products in unintended ways (misuse), Americans have the right to do so, so long as no harm is done to others.99

—North American Herbal Incense Trade Association, "NAHITA's Position on Laws That Limit American Consumer's Freedom of Choice," 2013. http://keepitlegal.org.

The North American Herbal Incense Trade Association is an organization of manufacturers and retailers that has opposed the Synthetic Drug Abuse Prevention Act of 2012 and other drug prohibition laws.

66 Many of the substances colloquially referred to as 'bath salts' all come in the form of an indistinct white powder. [New Zealand's] Psychoactive Substance Bill ensures that newly-legalized drugs are rigorously tested, have their contents clearly detailed on packaging, and that purity is guaranteed.99

—Avinash Tharoor, "5 Things We Can Learn from New Zealand's Innovative Law to Regulate New Drugs," *Huffington Post*, September 13, 2013. www.huffingtonpost.com.

Tharoor is a journalist and an intern at the Drug Policy Alliance.

66 Whether New Zealand's bold move does achieve the chief aim of any drug policy—keeping young people safe as possible from the dangers of drugs—remains to be seen.99

—Max Daly, "Not Regulating 'Legal Highs' Condemns Drug Users to Playing Russian Roulette," *Guardian* (Manchester), March 3, 2014. http://theguardian.com.

Daly is a journalist who covers social affairs and illegal drugs.

How Should Government Combat Use of Synthetic Drugs?

- Daniel Francis of the Retail Compliance Association estimates that synthetic drugs are a **$5 billion** annual retail market in the United States.

- Under the Synthetic Drug Abuse Prevention Act of 2012, it is illegal to manufacture or sell twenty-six specific substances found in bath salts and other synthetic drugs. First-time offenders could be sentenced to up to **20 years** in prison; repeat offenders could be sentenced to up to **30 years**.

- The first major law enforcement action in the United States against synthetic drugs occurred in July 2012. The DEA arrested ninety people around the country for the importation and distribution of synthetic marijuana (spice) and stimulants (bath salts). The DEA seized almost **5 million packets** of spice, **167,000 packets** of bath salts, and **$36 million** in cash.

- In 2011 the US Customs and Border Protection made **183** synthetic drug seizures. In 2012 the agency made **218** synthetic drug seizures.

- According to the United Nations Office on Drugs and Crime, in 2013 there were **693 online shops** for buying synthetic drugs (what the United Nations calls "new psychoactive substances"). This was up from **170** in 2010.

States Fight Synthetic Cathinones with New Laws

Most American states have passed laws that have outlawed at least some synthetic cathinones (the chemicals sold as bath salts). Many state laws simply list specific cathinones to be banned. However, makers of synthetic drugs often use slightly modified chemicals to technically comply with these laws. In response, some states have passed or modified their drug laws by using broader language that bans entire classes of synthetic cathinones.

Legend:
- States that have banned entire classes of synthetic cathinones
- States with legislation pending that would ban entire classes of synthetic cathinones
- States that have banned some specific synthetic cathinones

Source: National Alliance for Model State Drug Laws, "Substituted Cathinones," November 20, 2013. www.namsdl.org.

- According to the United Nations Office on Drugs and Crime, synthetic drugs in Europe were most popular in Poland, Great Britain, Latvia, and Ireland. More than **8 percent** of people aged fifteen to twenty-four in these countries have tried synthetic drugs.

- In October 2011 the Council of the European Union adopted a pact against synthetic drugs to help countries more effectively control production and trafficking of the drugs.

Online Drug Sellers Complicate Enforcement Efforts

The enforcement of local, national, and international laws against the selling of synthetic drugs is complicated by the existence of Internet shops. Many exist outside a specific government's jurisdiction, and when websites are successfully shut down by police raids, more spring up in their place. According to the European Monitoring Centre for Drugs and Drug Addiction, which has monitored places on the Internet where synthetic drugs can be purchased, the number of such shops in Europe has doubled since 2011.

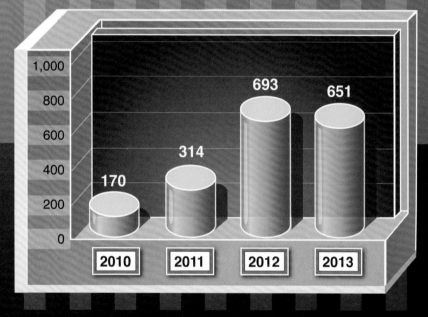

Number of Online Shops in Europe that Sell Synthetic Drugs

Source: European Monitoring Centre for Drugs and Addiction, "European Drug Report 2014: Trends and Developments," 2014.

- As of mid-2014 no drug had qualified for legal sale status in New Zealand.

- Louisiana was the first US state to pass legislation against bath salts, banning six synthetic cathinones in January 2011.

Synthetic Drug Cycle

This illustration depicts what some view as a problem with synthetic drug prohibition—the fact that new drugs are made to take their place, become popular, and are banned, only to begin the cycle anew.

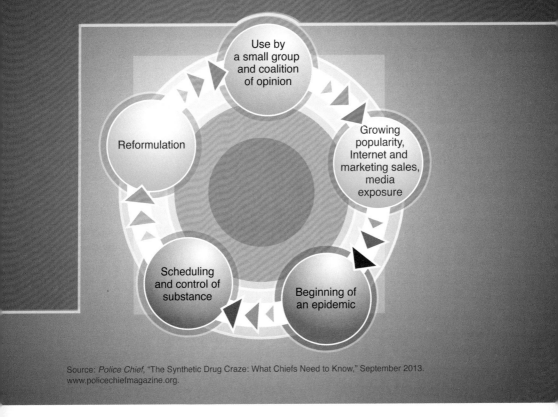

Source: *Police Chief*, "The Synthetic Drug Craze: What Chiefs Need to Know," September 2013. www.policechiefmagazine.org.

- Colorado has filed civil lawsuits against retailers of synthetic drugs under the Colorado Consumer Protection Act, charging retailers with misleading consumers and knowingly selling them harmful and/or illegal substances.

- Synthetic marijuana remains illegal even in Colorado and Washington, the two states that have legalized marijuana for recreational use.

- The US military has made synthetic drug use illegal under the Uniform Code of Military Justice.

Key People and Advocacy Groups

Jim Carlson: Carlson was an outspoken businessman who sold millions of dollars' worth of synthetic drugs at the Last Place on Earth, a popular head shop in Duluth, Minnesota. He sued the state of Minnesota after state agents raided his store in 2011, ran for president of the United States as the nominee of the Grassroots Party in 2012, and was convicted of multiple federal drug crimes in 2013.

Karen Dobner: Dobner became a political activist against synthetic drugs after her teen son died after smoking synthetic marijuana. She founded the To the Maximus Foundation to raise public awareness about synthetic drugs.

Drug Policy Alliance: This organization works to promote drug policies other than criminalization or prohibition; it has supported efforts to legalize marijuana and has opposed laws that ban synthetic drugs.

John W. Huffman: A chemistry professor at Clemson University, Huffman synthesized dozens of synthetic cannabinoids for research purposes.

National Institute on Drug Abuse: NIDA is an agency of the US Department of Health and Human Services that supports research on drug addiction and drug abuse in the United States.

Office of National Drug Control Policy: A part of the Executive Office of the President, this agency is responsible for directing the federal government's antidrug programs.

Mark Ryan: A physician who directs the Louisiana Poison Control Center, Ryan was among the first to document the significant rise in bath salts abuse and to alert health officials about it.

Alexander Shulgin: A California pharmacologist, Shulgin developed hundreds of synthetic psychoactive drugs, many of which he tested on himself. His books cataloging his research have been criticized by the DEA for teaching people how to make illegal drugs.

Spice Addiction Support: Spice Addiction Support is a website that provides a forum for people to write about their own experiences with spice, or synthetic marijuana.

United Nations Office on Drugs and Crime: This United Nations organization publishes materials on the proliferation of synthetic drugs worldwide, including the *World Drug Report*, an annual report on international drug trafficking.

Nora D. Volkow: The director of NIDA, Volkow has written and spoken frequently about the dangers of substance abuse among youth and the growing problem of synthetic drugs.

Chronology

1928
The first synthetic cathinone is produced by Russian scientists and is used as an antidepressant.

1995
Clemson University organic chemistry professor John W. Huffman creates a synthetic cannabinoid compound known as JWH-018.

1987
Chemist Richard A. Glennon publishes a paper in the journal *Pharmacology, Biochemistry and Behavior*, in which he describes his creation of a synthetic cathinone.

1970
Congress passes the Comprehensive Drug Abuse Prevention and Control Act (Controlled Substances Act), which establishes five schedules for the classification and control of drug substances that are subject to abuse.

1925   1960   1980   2000

1964
Scientists first isolate the psychoactive substance THC from the *Cannabis sativa* plant.

1986
Congress passes the Controlled Substances Analogue Enforcement Act, which makes it illegal to distribute drugs for human consumption that are chemically similar to chemical offshoots, or analogues, of existing Schedule I substances.

1993
Natural cathinone (from the khat plant) is banned by the DEA as a Schedule I substance.

1988
As part of research into medical marijuana and the endocannabinoid system, the synthetic cannabinoid HU-210 is developed at Hebrew University of Jerusalem.

1991
California pharmacologist Alexander Shulgin publishes a book called *PiHKAL: A Chemical Love Story* in which he reveals his formulas for numerous hallucinogenic synthetic drugs.

2005

The first mention of MDPV, a stimulant used in bath salts, is made on an Internet discussion forum on recreational drugs.

2010

Kansas, Louisiana, and other states ban synthetic cannabinoids, cathinones, and other chemicals used for synthetic drugs.

2008

European scientists isolate synthetic cannabinoids as being the active ingredient in spice; the US Customs and Border Protection seizes its first shipment of spice in Dayton, Ohio.

2012

President Barack Obama signs the Synthetic Drug Abuse Prevention Act into law, which permanently bans twenty-six synthetic drugs by classifying them as Schedule I controlled substances.

2005

2010

2007

Law enforcement officials in Germany seize and identify MDPV for the first time.

2011

The DEA orders a temporary ban on five synthetic cannabinoids and three synthetic cathinones.

2009

At least twenty-one countries in the European Union report the presence of synthetic marijuana. Some ban several synthetic cannabinoids, including JWH-018. However, other synthetic cannabinoids are developed to take their place to make spice.

2013

The DEA issues a temporary ban on 25I-NBOMe and two other synthetic phenethylamine hallucinogens.

2004

Spice (K2) is sold on the Internet for the first time.

2014

The DEA proposes adding four synthetic cannabinoids to its Schedule I listing of banned drugs.

Related Organizations

American Association of Poison Control Centers (AAPCC)
515 King St., Suite 510
Alexandria, VA 22314
phone: (703) 894-1858
e-mail: info@aapcc.org • website: www.aapcc.org

The AAPCC is the parent organization for fifty-seven poison control centers throughout the United States and maintains the country's only comprehensive poisoning surveillance database. Its website offers a large collection of data and statistics about synthetic drugs.

Council on Chemical Abuse
601 Penn St., Suite 600
Reading, PA 19601
phone: (610) 376-8669 • fax: (610) 376-8423
website: www.councilonchemicalabuse.org

The Council on Chemical Abuse serves as the coordinating agency for publicly supported programming on drug and alcohol abuse throughout Berks County, Pennsylvania. A number of articles and fact sheets about synthetic drugs are available through its website.

Drug Enforcement Administration (DEA)
2401 Jefferson Davis Hwy.
Alexandria, VA 22301
phone: (202) 307-1000; toll-free: (800) 332-4288
website: www.justice.gov/dea

The DEA enforces federal laws against the trafficking of illegal drugs and assists state and local law enforcement officers. Its website offers numerous publications about bath salts and other synthetic drugs.

Drug Free America Foundation
5999 Central Ave., Suite 301
Saint Petersburg, FL 33710
phone: (727) 828-0211 • fax: (727) 828-0212
e-mail: webmaster@dfaf.org • website: www.dfaf.org

The Drug Free America Foundation is a drug prevention and policy organization. Its website has a search engine that produces numerous articles about bath salts and other synthetic drugs, as well as links to a site for young people titled Students Taking Action Not Drugs (STAND).

Drug Policy Alliance

131 W. Thirty-Third St., 15th Floor
New York, NY 10001
phone: (212) 613-8020 • fax: (212) 613-8021
e-mail: nyc@drugpolicy.org • website: www.drugpolicy.org

The Drug Policy Alliance promotes alternatives to drug prohibition policies. Its website features drug facts, statistics, information about drug laws, and a search engine that produces a number of articles about synthetic drugs.

National Institute on Drug Abuse (NIDA)

National Institutes of Health
6001 Executive Blvd., Room 5213
Bethesda, MD 20892-9561
phone: (301) 443-1124
e-mail: information@nida.nih.gov • website: www.drugabuse.gov

NIDA supports research efforts and ensures the rapid dissemination of research to improve drug abuse prevention, treatment, and policy. The website links to a separate NIDA for Teens site, which is designed especially for teenagers and provides information about illicit drugs, including bath salts and other synthetic drugs.

Office of National Drug Control Policy (ONDCP)

750 Seventeenth St. NW
Washington, DC 20503
phone: (800) 666-3332 • fax: (202) 395-6708
e-mail: ondcp@ncjrs.org • website: www.whitehouse.gov/ondcp

A component of the Executive Office of the President, the ONDCP is responsible for directing the federal government's antidrug programs. Information about bath salts and other synthetic drugs can be accessed on its website.

Partnership for Drug-Free Kids

352 Park Ave. S., 9th Floor
New York, NY 10010
phone: (212) 922-1560 • fax: (212) 922-1570
website: www.drugfree.org

This nonprofit organization, formerly known as the Partnership for a Drug-Free America, is dedicated to helping parents and families solve the problem of teenage substance abuse. Its website offers a wide variety of informative publications, including *Parents 360 Synthetic Drugs: A Guide for Parents and Other Influencers.*

StoptheDrugWar.org

PO Box 9853
Washington, DC 20016
phone: (202) 293-8340 • fax: (202) 293-8344
website: www.stopthedrugwar.org

Stopthedrugwar.org works to end drug prohibition worldwide and to promote policies that minimize harms caused by criminalization of drugs. Its website provides updates on laws and government policies affecting the availability of synthetic drugs.

Substance Abuse and Mental Health Services Administration (SAMHSA)

1 Choke Cherry Rd.
Rockville, MD 20857
phone: (877) 726-4727 • fax: (240) 221-4292
e-mail: samhsainfo@samhsa.hhs.gov • website: www.samhsa.gov

SAMHSA's mission is to reduce the impact of substance abuse and mental illness on America's communities. The site offers a wealth of information about substance abuse, and numerous publications related to bath salts and other synthetic drugs can be produced through its search engine.

To the Maximus Foundation

1120 Grenada Dr.

Aurora, IL 60506

phone: (630) 892-3629

e-mail: info@2themax.org • website: http://2themax.org

Created in memory of a young man who died after using synthetic marijuana, the To the Maximus Foundation is committed to education about and awareness of the dangers of synthetic drugs. Its website offers news releases, fact sheets, testimonials, and links to other resources.

For Further Research

Books

Paul I. Dargon and David M. Wood, *Novel Psychoactive Substances.* Waltham, MA: Academic Press, 2013.

Raymond Goldberg, *Drugs Across the Spectrum.* Belmont, CA: Wadsworth, 2012.

Terrence L. Gray and Sage F. Evans, eds., *Synthetic Drugs: Scope and Trends in Synthetic Cannabinoids and Stimulants.* Hauppauge, NY: Nova Science Publishers, 2012.

Mark J. Minelli, *Drugs of Abuse: A Quick Information Guide.* Champaign, IL: Stipes, 2013.

Peggy J. Parks, *Bath Salts and Other Synthetic Drugs.* San Diego, CA: ReferencePoint, 2013.

Mike Power, *Drugs 2.0: The Web Revolution That's Changing How the World Gets High.* London, UK: Portobello, 2013.

Howard Samuels with Jane O'Boyle, *Alive Again: Recovering from Alcoholism and Drug Addiction.* Hoboken, NJ: Wiley, 2013.

Periodicals

Carrie Arnold, "The New Danger of Synthetic Drugs," *Lancet*, July 6, 2013.

Emily K. Dye, "The Synthetic Drug Craze: What Chiefs Need to Know," *Police Chief*, September 2013.

Economist, "Bath Salts: The Synthetic Scare," August 4, 2012.

Eliza Gray, "The Rise of Fake Pot," *Time*, April 21, 2014.

Vanessa Grigoriadis, "Travels in the New Psychedelic Bazaar," *New York*, April 7, 2013.

Ashley Mateo, "I Over Dosed on Synthetic Drugs!," *Seventeen*, June/July 2012.

Jacob Sullivan, "Bath Salts Face Off: Synthetic Drug Ban," *Reason*, October 2012.

Jennifer Van Pelt, "Synthetic Drugs—Fake Substances, Real Dangers," *Social Work Today*, July/August 2012.

Teri Moser Woo et al., "How High Do They Look? Identification and Treatment of Common Ingestions in Adolescents," *Journal of Pediatric Health Care*, March–April 2013.

Internet Sources

Mary Bellis, "Synthetic Marijuana: Organic Chemist John W. Huffman Invented the Formula for Synthetic Marijuana," About.com. http://inventors.about.com/od/hstartinventors/a/Synthetic-Marijuana.htm.

Stephen Bright and Monica Barratt, "Explainer: What Is NBOMe?," *Conversation*, August 23, 2013. http://theconversation.com/explainer-what-is-nbome-16950.

Glenn Duncan, "Comprehensive Drug Information on Synthetic Cannabinoids—'Spice' and 'K2,'" Hunterdon Drug Awareness Program, June 29, 2012. www.hdap.org/spice.html.

Tricia Escobedo, "What You Need to Know About Synthetic Drugs," CNN Health, September 13, 2013. www.cnn.com/2013/09/13/health/synthetic-drugs-7-things.

Dirk Hanson, "The Year in Synthetic Drugs," *Salon*, December 26, 2012. www.salon.com/2012/12/26/the_year_in_synthetic_drugs.

Olga Khazan, "Synthetic Drugs Are Multiplying Too Fast for Regulators to Outlaw Them," *Atlantic*, June 27, 2013. www.theatlantic.com/international/archive/2013/06/synthetic-drugs-are-multiplying-too-fast-for-regulators-to-outlaw-them/277321.

Jenny Marder, "The Drug That Never Lets Go," *PBS NewsHour*, September 20, 2012. www.pbs.org/newshour/multimedia/bath-salts.

Beth A. Rutkowksi "Will They Turn You into a Zombie? What SUD Treatment Providers Need to Know About Synthetic Drugs," UCLA Integrated Substance Abuse Programs, March 15, 2013. www.uclaisap.org/slides/presentations-psattc-sapc.html.

Phillip Smith, "President Obama Signs Knee-Jerk Ban on Synthetic Drugs like 'Bath Salts' and 'Fake Weed,'" AlterNet, July 10, 2012. www.alter net.org/story/156254/obama_signs_knee-jerk_ban_on_synthetic _drugs_like_%22bath_salts%22_and_%22fake_weed%22.

Maia Szalavitz, "The Cannabis Cannibal? Miami Face-Eater Didn't Take 'Bath Salts,'" *Time*, June 27, 2012. http://healthland.time.com /2012/06/27/the-cannabis-cannibal-miami-face-eater-didnt-take -bath-salts.

Source Notes

Overview

1. Quoted in Christian Boone, "Teen's Death Officially Linked to Synthetic Pot," *Atlanta Journal-Constitution*, June 5, 2012. www.ajc.com.
2. Partnership at Drugfree.org, "Parents 360 Synthetic Drugs: Bath Salts, K2/Spice," community education presentation, February 16, 2012. www.drugfree.org.
3. Quoted in Matt McMillen, "'Bath Salts' Drug Trend: Expert Q&A," WebMD Feature, February 26, 2013. www.webmd.com.
4. Dirk Hanson, "Are Bath Salts Addictive?," *Addiction Inbox* (blog), June 26, 2012. http://addiction-dirkh.blogspot.com.
5. Hanson, "Are Bath Salts Addictive?"
6. Howard Samuelson, "Facts About Spice Addiction," Hills Treatment Center. www.thehillscenter.com.
7. Quoted in Alexandra Lundahl, "Largo Couple Struggles with Daughter's Addiction," *TBNweekly.com*, August 21, 2012. www.tbnweekly.com.
8. Emily Ethridge, "Lawmakers Attempt to Keep Up with Synthetic Drugs," *Roll Call*, October 28, 2013. www.rollcall.com.
9. Quoted in Ethridge, "Lawmakers Attempt to Keep Up with Synthetic Drugs."
10. Quoted in Ethridge, "Lawmakers Attempt to Keep Up with Synthetic Drugs."

What Are Synthetic Drugs?

11. Jason Jerry et al., "Synthetic Legal Intoxicating Drugs: The Emerging 'Incense' and 'Bath Salt' Phenomenon," *Cleveland Clinic Journal of Medicine*, April 2012, p. 259.
12. Jeffrey Post, "Spice Smoking Causes Psychosis in Healthy Users," Trident Team Safety, June 14, 2012. www.tridentteamsafety.com.
13. Drug Enforcement Administration Office of Diversion Control, "25I-NBOMe, 25C-NBOMe, and 25B-NBOMe," November 2013. www.deadiversion.usdoj.gov.
14. White House Office of National Drug Control Policy, "Synthetic Drugs (a.k.a. Spice, Bath Salts, etc.)," fact sheet, 2013. www.whitehouse.gov.

Do Synthetic Drugs Pose a Significant Public Health Threat?

15. Quoted in Katie Kerwin McCrimmon, "Synthetic Pot Generates National Warning to ER Docs," Health News Colorado, January 22, 2014. www.healthnewscolorado.org.
16. Quoted in National Institute on Drug Abuse, "I-Science: NIDA's Look into What We Still Need to Know About Synthetic Cannabinoids," transcript, September 2013. www.drugabuse.gov.
17. Quoted in Florida Department of Health in Polk County, "Dangers of Using Synthetic Illegal Drugs," press release, June 9, 2014. www.mypolkhealth.net.
18. Quoted in Arshid Mir et al., "Myocardial Infarction Associated with Use of Synthetic Cannabinoid K2," *Pediatrics*, December 2011. http://pediatrics.aappublications.org.

19. David DiSalvo, "The Straight Dope on What Bath Salts Do to Your Brain and Why They're Dangerous," *Forbes*, June 5, 2012. www.forbes.com.

20. National Institute on Drug Abuse, "Synthetic Cathinones ('Bath Salts')," November 2012. www.drugabuse.gov.

21. American College of Emergency Physicians, "Synthetic Drugs Fact Sheet," 2012. http://newsroom.acep.org.

22. Vikas Mangewala et al., "Bath-Salts-Induced Psychosis," *Innovations in Clinical Neuroscience*, February 2013, p. 10.

23. Mangewala et al., "Bath-Salts-Induced Psychosis."

24. Quoted in CBS Miami, "Causeway Cannibal Identified; Fears Grow over Drug Possibly Involved," May 28, 2012. http://miami.cbslocal.com.

25. American College of Emergency Physicians, "Synthetic Drugs Fact Sheet."

26. Teri Moser Woo et al., "How High Do They Look? Identification and Treatment of Common Ingestions in Adolescents," *Journal of Pediatric Health Care*, March–April 2013, p. 135.

27. Quoted in Alexis Gray, "The Legal Drug Epidemic No One Is Talking About," *Northattan*, October 7, 2013. http://northattan.com.

28. Quoted in Larry Oakes, "Users Play Chemical Roulette," *Minneapolis (MN) Star Tribune*, September 8, 2011. www.startribune.com.

29. Quoted in University of Colorado School of Medicine, "More Illness from Synthetic Marijuana Likely," press release, January 22, 2014. www.eurekalert.org.

How Addictive Are Synthetic Drugs?

30. Kelly, "Spice Has Done Nothing but Destroy My Life," Spice Addiction Support, April 16, 2014. http://spiceaddictionsupport.org.

31. Kelly, "Spice Has Done Nothing but Destroy My Life."

32. Drug Policy Alliance, "K2/Spice: Establish Regulations But Don't Criminalize It," 2010. www.drugpolicy.org.

33. National Institute on Drug Abuse, "Spice: ('Synthetic Marijuana')," December 2012. www.drugabuse.gov.

34. Quoted in McMillen, "Bath Salts Drug Trend."

35. Nora D. Volkow, preface to *The Science of Addiction*, National Institute on Drug Abuse, July 2014. www.drugabuse.gov.

36. American Society of Addiction Medicine, "Public Policy Statement—Definition of Addiction," April 19, 2011. www.asam.org

37. Quoted in Jennifer Van Pelt, "Synthetic Drugs—Fake Substance, Real Dangers," *Social Work Today*, July/August 2012, p. 12.

38. Quoted in Melanie Haiken, "Bath Salts a Deadly New Drug with a Deceptively Innocent Name," *Forbes*, June 4, 2012. www.forbes.com.

39. Quoted in Sharon Kay, "Woman, 21, Shares Her Struggle to Overcome Addiction to Bath Salts," KCAL9 news, October 26, 2012. http://losangeles.cbslocal.com.

40. Alan Stevens, *Understanding Addiction to Bath Salts*. Highland Park, NJ: Pomerantz, 2014, p. 10.

41. Alice G. Walton, "Synthetic Drug 'Bath Salts' Trumps Methamphetamine in Addictiveness, Study Finds," *Forbes*, July 10, 2013. www.forbes.com.

How Should Government Combat Use of Synthetic Drugs?

42. Quoted in KGO-TV, "DEA Wages War on Synthetic Drugs Sold on Internet," December 18, 2013. http://abc7news.com/archive/9365506/.

43. Title 21 USC § 813.

44. Hari Sathappan, "The Federal Controlled Substances Analogue Act: An Antiquated Solution Meets an Evolving Problem," *Amici Blog, Ohio State Journal of Criminal Law*, November 21, 2012. http://moritzlaw.osu.edu.

45. Quoted in John Femino, "Take Action: Ban Dangerous Synthetic Drugs," *Asamagazine*, January 30, 2014. www.asam.org.

46. Sam Friedman, "New 'Spice' Ban in Alaska Fines Stores That Sell Synthetic Drugs," Newsminor.com, July 16, 2014. www.newsminor.com.

47. Quoted in Drug Policy Alliance, "Today: U.S. Senate Hearing on Synthetic Drugs Offers Failed Drug War Policies of the Past," press release, September 25, 2013. www.drugpolicy.org.

48. Drug Policy Alliance, "K2/Spice: Establish Regulations But Don't Criminalize It."

49. Eric E. Sterling, "Horrifying New Drugs! Does New Zealand's New Synthetic Drug Law Offer a Safer Way Forward?," *Huffington Post*, October 15, 2013. www.huffingtonpost.com.

50. Quoted in Drug Policy Alliance, "Legislation to Ban K2/Spice, 'Bath Salts' and Other Synthetic Drugs Sailing Through Congress Today," July 28, 2011. www.drugpolicy.org.

51. Quoted in Matt Ferner, "Should Synthetic Marijuana Be Banned in States Where Real Pot Is Now Legal?," *Huffington Post*, September 3, 2013.

52. Elaine Gottlieb, "Cannabis: A Danger to the Adolescent Brain—How Pediatricians Can Address Marijuana Use," Massachusetts Child Psychiatry Access Project, August 2012. www.mcpap.com.

53. Francesca Liquori, "Education and Prevention Initiatives as Necessary Tools to Combat Synthetic Drug Abuse," *NAAGazette*, May 29, 2014. www.naag.org.

List of Illustrations

Index

Note: Boldface page numbers indicate illustrations.

About the Author

William Dudley is a substitute teacher and writer whose works include *Antidepressants* and *Thinking Critically: Stem Cell Research*. He holds a BA in English from Beloit College. He lives in San Diego, California.